RAWvolution

MATT AMSDEN

RAWvolution
Gourmet Living Cuisine

REGAN

An Imprint of HarperCollins*Publishers*

HarperCollins books may be purchased for educational, business, or sales promotional use. For information please write: Special Markets Department, HarperCollins Publishers Inc., 10 East 53rd Street, New York, NY 10022.

FIRST EDITION

Photography by ANDREA GÓMEZ

Designed by JUDITH STAGNITTO ABBATE / ABBATE DESIGN

Food Styling by LIESL MAGGIORE

Printed on acid-free paper
Library of Congress Cataloging-in-Publication Data
Amsden, Matt.
    RAWvolution : gourmet living cuisine / Matt Amsden.
       p. cm.
    ISBN-13: 978-0-06-084318-2
    ISBN-10: 0-06-084318-7
    1.   Cookery (Natural foods) 2.   Raw foods.   I. Title.
    TX741.A573 2006
    641.5'63—dc22   2006043763
06 07 08 09 10 QT 10 9 8 7 6 5 4 3 2 1

This book is dedicated to JANABAI,
the love of my life,
my twin flame,
my soul mate,
etc., etc., etc.

Contents

MY BACK Pages: How I Went Raw

I eat the best food in the world—foods like tomatoes, grown from heirloom seeds and ripened in the sun of central California; olive oil, stone-pressed in Spain; and vanilla beans, hand-harvested from vanilla orchids in Madagascar. And, even better, *you* can eat them, too!

The amazing culinary delights I've created from these incredible ingredients are the inspiration for this book. Vine-ripened fruit, crisp garden vegetables, crunchy seeds and nuts, fresh herbs, and gourmet spices . . . The ingredients are simple, organic, and vegetarian, but the results are rich and gorgeous.

Another amazing thing about these dishes is that they are never cooked. No ingredient is ever exposed to heat much higher than body temperature. This creates food with the taste of uncompromised freshness and vitality, dishes that are vibrant and beautiful, and meals that leave you feeling light and energized. If you think eating raw food is a life of apple slices and celery sticks, I urge you to try the recipes in this book. You will see that it can be so much more!

The raw food that I ate as a kid growing up in Ontario, Canada, was modest at best. Fruit consisted of the occasional spotted banana, a fistful of green grapes, or a

soft apple. Even carrot and celery sticks were really just a vehicle for ranch dressing. Like most families, we also had our share of meat, cheese, bread, milk, cookies, cereal, and potato chips.

Looking back, it's hard for me to believe that was my lifestyle. I have since discovered these foods are quite difficult to digest, contribute little nutritionally, and are even linked directly to diseases plaguing modern society.

These days I am more likely to be eating a creamy cherimoya, or a little yellow honey mango from Mexico, or a perfectly ripe Cal Red peach from the lush Sacramento River delta in northern California. Wow, life tastes good! Wow, how things change.

It all started one July morning. I was driving home after the night shift at a factory where I molded plastic parts for automobiles. I tuned the radio of my '82

Cutlass Supreme to the Howard Stern show, as I usually did. The first thing I heard was a guest on the show describing the harmful effects of cooked food on one's sexual health. My ears perked up! It made sense, too. Eat heavy, highly processed foods that hamper circulation and blood flow, and soon you're not half the man you used to be. There were two words the guest mentioned that *really* caught my attention, though: raw food. The first thing I did after pulling into the driveway of my house was log onto the Internet and type in "www.rawfood.com." I did not take a shower, or go to bed. I had been up all night trimming plastic bumper covers and all I could think about were those two words, "raw food." Something implored me to investigate this right away. It sounded so radical and yet so logical. I read every word on that website and was amazed at the information that was revealed. The food I had been eating my whole life, foods that I had fully accepted as being completely healthy, were now questionable. This approach to eating was different from anything I had ever heard. It awakened something inside of me and instantly set my life on a new course.

The guest on Stern's show that day was David Wolfe (whom I have since worked and become friends with). I ordered a copy of the book he was promoting, *Nature's First Law: The Raw-Food Diet* (Maul Brothers, 1997). In it, David and his coauthors spoke of adopting a diet of 100 percent raw foods. I read that book cover to cover and as I closed it, I said to myself, "This is what I am going to do."

That was in 1998, and since then that is what I have done. I began eating uncooked fruits, vegetables, nuts, and seeds—exclusively.

This book is meant to inspire you, as I was inspired. It is meant to assist you in incorporating raw foods into your life to whatever degree appeals to you. It's about looking at the food you eat and determining whether or not it is the best food on the planet. That's what you deserve and that is what you have available to you—the very best food on the planet!

I have since found many ways to convert these simple ingredients into mouthwatering culinary works of art. This book is the "fruit" of those labors.

When I serve someone my Big Matt with Cheese (page 125), their reaction is usually something like, "Wow, it has all the elements of a great burger without the fat or greasiness!" *That* is what I strive for.

Anyone can chop veggies, dress them with oil and vinegar, and call themselves a raw food chef. My goal, however, has been to create gourmet recipes of the highest order from simple, wholesome ingredients that can be duplicated in your kitchen. It has been my passion to create recipes that are truly healthy, amazingly delicious, visually stunning, and accessible for nearly anyone to prepare.

I love exotic, hard-to-find ingredients as much as the next chef. But here I chose to give you recipes that you can make at home—*and* be thrilled with the results.

HAVE FUN!

ONE

THE RAW &
the Cooked

An Introduction to Raw, Living Foods

WHAT ARE "RAW" OR "LIVING" FOODS?

Raw or living foods are those that have not been exposed to temperatures above 105° Fahrenheit, thus maintaining their enzymatic and nutritional properties.

WHAT IS ORGANIC FOOD?

Organic food is, in general, food that is grown without the use of artificial pesticides, herbicides, and genetically modified organisms (GMOs). Purchasing food that is marked "Certified Organic" ensures that it was grown in accordance with these parameters.

WHAT ARE "VEGETARIANISM" AND "VEGANISM"?

Vegetarians eat a diet based on foods from plants, including fruits, vegetables, grains, nuts, and seeds.

With the myriad of unnatural and synthetic pesticides, herbicides, insecticides, and fungicides used in today's commercial factory farming, it is easy to understand why eating only organically grown produce is a good idea. And although years ago vegetarianism was regarded as fringe and idealistic, practiced only by extremists and militant animal rights activists, mainstream consciousness has, for the most part, come to accept even those of us who have chosen to follow the more "radical" vegan lifestyle.

Vegans exclude all things of animal origin from their diet. They also choose not to use or wear anything made from, or containing, animal by-products, including leather, silk, fur, and feathers.

WHY DO YOU EAT ONLY RAW FOODS?

This is a question I am often asked when explaining that I eat only uncooked vegetables, fruit, nuts, and seeds.

Why, then, might *you* choose to eat raw foods?

1. Unbelievable Flavor!

The flavor of raw foods is so fresh and alive because they are as nature intended, full of living water and life force. If you have ever enjoyed a soft, ripe peach at the peak of its growing season, you know this.

After a short time of eating raw foods, you will feel as if your palate has been cleansed from the inside out, and you will be able to taste things as you have never tasted them before. I remember noticing this when I began eating raw foods. I had always loved watermelon, but experiencing the depth of the flavor was now almost a moving experience; it was unbelievable that something could taste so good. Sweet things will taste even sweeter, and foods that had once been bitter, like dark salad greens, will begin to taste wholesome and nourishing. An actual physical transformation will occur, and it will allow you to enjoy what you eat even more. What a nice benefit.

2. Living Water!

You are what you eat. If your body is over 70 percent water, shouldn't your food choices mirror this?

When you are cooking, the steam you see is the water leaving your food!

Doctors and health professionals suggest we drink eight to ten glasses of water each day. Whether they realize it or not, this is necessary largely because people are cooking the natural water out of their food. Eat half of a watermelon and tell me if you're thirsty.

Everything you put in your stomach needs to be turned into liquid to be digested. What do you think is more easily turned into liquid, a cucumber or a pork chop? Not only does cooked food do nothing to provide your body with much-needed water; it also dehydrates you further as your body attempts to digest it. In raw food preparation, we sometimes use a food dehydrator. This, of course, also dehydrates food; however, it is used mainly to create texture and represents a small percentage of raw cuisine.

3. Real Vitamins and Minerals

Vitamins and minerals are a major focus in the study of nutrition (the study of nutrients required by the body). I'm not talking about synthetic pills made in a factory; I'm talking about the real thing—like the vitamin C in bell peppers, and the calcium in fresh spinach.

A well-balanced diet of raw plant foods contains the full complement of vitamins and minerals necessary for good nutrition, while cooking destroys over 80 percent of a food's nutritive value. Can you afford 80 percent less nutrition than is naturally found in your food?

4. Enzymes

Enzymes are responsible for every metabolic process that takes place in your body, from digestion to cell repair. Cooking destroys up to 100 percent of the enzymes in your food. One hundred percent!

When you consume foods that are rich in enzymes, it practically digests itself, leaving you with a surplus of energy to do what you love. How much more fun is yoga than lying on the couch, digesting a turkey?

5. Examples in Nature

Raw, organic plant foods are by far the most abundant foods on the planet, which I think is a clear sign that they are meant to be our foods of choice.

The truth is, eating raw foods is not a diet; it is a lifestyle. It can be described as a diet only in the sense that whatever one eats is one's diet. In that way, we are all on a diet of some kind—and some diets are healthy while others are not.

When a koala chooses to eat eucalyptus or when a tiger eats only prey it has taken down with its own jaws, it is not out of a desire to follow a prescribed diet. Wild animals are drawn instinctively to the foods that are fresh and abundant in their area and that support their total well-being.

Gorillas need not decide what to eat; their surroundings and instincts guide them to the perfect choices for their bodies and environment. They are not concerned with protein and get plenty from the green leaves they eat almost exclusively.

If you look at your surroundings—not your temporary, modern, artificial surroundings, such as grocery stores and fast-food restaurants, but rather your *true*, natural surroundings—you will see that it is filled with wild edible plants, herbs, grasses, and fruiting trees.

No creature, whether it ate plants or other animals, ever chose to cook its food. What would be the benefit? It is time to look at the idea that there is in fact no benefit to cooking your food. We do it out of habit or some unrealistic fear of germs or microbes. Even Louis Pasteur, inventor of the still widely accepted process of pasteurization (which is thought to make milk and fruit juices "safe" to drink by exposing them to unnaturally high temperatures) acknowledged his theory as erroneous at the end of his life.

6. Quality of Life

The way that you feel when you begin to eat a diet of primarily raw, living, organic foods is more than enough to keep you doing it. Not a lot of discipline or reaffirmations of facts is necessary once your energy and mental clarity have sharpened to a degree that you have not experienced since childhood. Your body will change, gravitating toward its natural weight.

Since "going raw" in 1998, my physical energy and stamina have increased, I require less sleep, and can function at an optimal rate for a much longer period of time. I am never ill, I've forgotten what a headache feels like, any wounds heal much more quickly, I am physically stronger, and my reflexes are incredible! Even my vision, hearing, and sense of smell have improved.

Once, a friend and I were not sure if Santa Monica's outdoor farmers' market would be open because it was the Saturday of a holiday weekend. As we stepped outside of my home, I told her that I knew for sure that it was open because I could actually smell the abundance of produce. The market was more than ten blocks away!

A pure diet leads one toward a more natural lifestyle.

You will find yourself wanting to spend more time in nature. A deep, full-body tan may follow.

7. Mental Outlook and
Spiritual Progression

When you change your diet, you really become a different person, and your world seems to become a different place. Synchronicities begin to happen more and more often, which may be a sign from the universe that you are on the right path. Animals will begin to interact with you in a different way, as they are no longer afraid that you may eat them. Your outlook on the day—not to mention the state of the world and society—will shift. You may find yourself being drawn to an orange or yellow shirt, even though you have always hated those colors.

The way that you deal with your family, friends, and colleagues will also evolve. You may find that you are becoming more compassionate, thoughtful, considerate, understanding, and empathetic. Others will notice these changes in you as well.

You can clear the mental fog that poor eating habits create and think much more clearly. The fatigue and lethargy caused by a poor diet is replaced with energy and vigor.

Your temperament may change. If you have been timid, you may begin to take more risks. If you have been reckless, you may recognize the value of this wonderful existence and slow down a little.

You truly are what you eat. You can choose to be light, vibrant, fresh, and alive, or you can be dry, dull, gray, heavy, and lifeless, like the standard American fare.

When you choose a diet that is compassionate toward animals and nature, nature responds by being kind and compassionate in return. This is not just a lovely sentiment or New Age hocus-pocus; it is an irrefutable law of cause and effect.

No single thing affects our lives or the world we live in as much as eating, something that most of us do at least three times every single day. Once the way in which you feed yourself changes or evolves, your entire existence evolves.

When your body and mind are free of pollutants, you become a clear channel for receiving information from the universe. There is no longer anything to prevent it. This demonstrates a direct and authentic intention to the universe.

When you become connected with the inner workings of the universe, you allow yourself the opportunity to tap into a consciousness that you have never

known and yet always known. The simplicity of feeding yourself from only the plants of the earth is, paradoxically, one of the most profound things you can do.

Your body is your temple. Once your temple is clean and pure, there is space for divinity, insight, and virtue to reside. A temple so full of waste is unreceptive to the subtleties of the body's divine wisdom, and is therefore unreceptive to the subtleties of existence itself.

Cleanliness *is* next to godliness, and the control of one's appetite is a true hallmark of enlightenment and immortality.

TWO

HOW TO
Use This Book

The legend that appears on every recipe page tells you, at a glance, what is involved in preparing each dish. This key allows you to decide "what to make for lunch" without having to read a whole book first!

The top right quadrant of the key contains a number—1, 2, or 3—indicating the recipe's relative level of complexity. While none of these recipes is difficult to make, some are simpler than others. Below, you'll find a short description of what each number involves, and what each icon symbolizes.

1 These recipes are the easiest to prepare because they contain fewer ingredients, require less equipment, or take less time to make. Although some of the recipes in this category have lengthy ingredient lists, often you will only need to put them in a blender and turn it on.

2 These may require more than one appliance or incorporate a greater number of steps.

3 These involve more appliances, require a little more time to create, and/or involve some soaking and dehydrating.

ICONS

HIGH-SPEED BLENDER

FOOD DEHYDRATOR

FOOD PROCESSOR

JUICER

MY FAVORITE RECIPE in each section!

Learn more about these appliances in the Glossary on page 195.

THREE

STOCKING YOUR
Raw Kitchen

always say, "The easiest shortcut to making great-tasting food is using the best ingredients." Keep that in mind when you're at the health food store! While you shouldn't need to spend a fortune to eat wonderful food, some-times a few extra dollars means a world of improvement in quality. Invest in your health, and the returns will filter into all aspects of your life.

Many of the following items can be found at your local health food store or online at www.rawfood.com. If you're not sure what an ingredient is, refer to the Glossary on page 195.

CONDIMENTS

○ Apple cider vinegar
  (look for organic, raw, unfiltered)
○ Nama Shoyu
○ Olive oil (look for organic,
  cold-pressed, or better still—
  stone-pressed)
○ Sea salt
○ Ume vinegar

NUTS (LOOK FOR ORGANIC, RAW, UNSALTED)

○ Almonds
○ Cashews
○ Macadamia nuts
○ Pecans
○ Pine nuts
○ Walnuts

SEEDS (LOOK FOR ORGANIC, RAW, UNSALTED)

○ Flax seeds
○ Hemp seeds
○ Pumpkin seeds
○ Sesame seeds (white and black)
○ Sunflower seeds

NUT AND SEED BUTTERS (LOOK FOR ORGANIC, RAW, OR COLD-PRESSED)

○ Almond butter
○ Cacao butter
○ Coconut butter (sometimes called
  "coconut oil")
○ Tahini

SEAWEED

○ Dulse flakes or granules
○ Whole-leaf dulse
○ Nori (raw nori is black, toasted nori
  is green)
○ Wakame

SPICES (LOOK FOR ORGANIC)

○ Apple pie spice
○ Black pepper
○ Cayenne
○ Chili powder
○ Cinnamon
○ Coriander
○ Cumin
○ Curry powder
○ Garam masala
○ Nutmeg
○ Turmeric

(continued)

SWEETENERS AND DRIED FRUIT
(LOOK FOR ORGANIC)

○ Agave nectar (look for raw)

○ Carob powder (look for raw)

○ Dried coconut

○ Goji berries

○ Lucuma powder

○ Dried mango

○ Mesquite powder

○ Raisins

○ Sun-dried tomatoes

○ Vanilla bean

OTHER FOODS (LOOK FOR ORGANIC)

○ Cacao nibs or powder

○ Greek olives (look for sun-dried olives, cured in sea salt)

○ Green powder

○ Hemp protein powder

○ Italian olives (look for sun-dried olives, cured in sea salt)

○ Maca root powder

○ Stone-ground mustard

○ Spirulina

○ Pure water (filtered, distilled, reverse osmosis, or artesian spring)

APPLIANCES

- Blender, preferably Vita-Mix
- Food dehydrator, preferably Excalibur
- Food processor
- Juicer, preferably Green Star

MISCELLANEOUS EQUIPMENT

- Chef's knife
- Garlic press
- Mandoline slicer
- Nut-milk bag
- Pastry bag
- Spatula
- Spirooli Slicer
- Vegetable peeler

FOUR

GOOD MORNING,
Good Morning
Breakfasts

One of the questions I am asked most often by people who are new to the raw foods lifestyle is "What do you eat for breakfast?" I use breakfast as a time to get all of my nutritional supplements at once by combining them in what I call a Super-Food Shake (page 34)," an amazing drink made in the blender. In the raw food world, nutritional supplements are actually foods—"super-foods," really. In addition to being nutritional powerhouses, they actually taste good, even on their own! In this section, you will find the recipe for the drink I have every morning, and a few other great ways to start your day.

●　　●　　●

Berry and Nut
Breakfast Bar

Makes approximately 18 bars

A SATISFYING BREAKFAST treat that combines the sweetness of berries with the heartiness of nuts.

    2 cups raw almonds
    1 cup raw walnuts
    ¾ cup flax seeds
    2 cups fresh strawberries, raspberries, and/or blueberries
    1 cup raisins

Using a food processor, grind the almonds and walnuts coarsely, and then transfer the nuts to a large mixing bowl. Powder the flax seeds in a high-speed blender (or a spice or coffee grinder) and place in a small bowl. Liquefy the fresh berries in a blender, then add the flax powder to the blended berries and blend again. Add the resulting berry mixture to the ground nuts, along with the raisins, and mix well with a wooden spoon.

Spread the mixture evenly on a Teflex-lined dehydrator tray to a thickness of approximately 1 inch. Dehydrate at 100°F for 12 hours. Flip the tray over onto a work surface and gently peel the Teflex sheet off of the berry and nut mixture. Return the mixture to the dehydrator for another 12 hours. Once dehydrated, cut into 18 equal pieces (make 2 cuts horizontally, and 5 cuts vertically).

Milk It:
Vanilla Nut Milk

Serves 1 to 2

A CREAMY almond nut milk, flavored with a fresh vanilla bean and sweetened with agave nectar.

> 3 ½ cups Thai coconut water
> 1 cup raw hemp seeds or almonds
> ¼ to ⅓ cup agave nectar
> Pinch of sea salt
> Tiny seeds of 1 vanilla bean

In a high-speed blender, combine the coconut water and the hemp seeds or almonds and blend until smooth. If you are using almonds, strain the mixture through a nut-milk bag and discard the pulp, then return the strained milk to the blender. Add the agave nectar, sea salt, and vanilla seeds to the milk in the blender, and blend for approximately 30 seconds, or until the mixture is completely smooth. Chill and serve.

VARIATION:
If you want real chocolate milk, add ½ cup of cacao nibs or powder and 2 tablespoons of carob along with the agave and vanilla seeds, and blend.

Shake Your Money Maker:
Super-Food Shake

Serves 1 to 2

THIS HIGH-OCTANE breakfast beverage containing more than half a dozen super-foods will have you shakin' your money maker until lunch.

Water and flesh of 2 Thai coconuts

½ cup agave nectar (optional)

3 tablespoons carob powder

¼ cup Goji berries

¼ cup cacao nibs or powder

½ cup hemp seeds or raw cashews

¼ cup raw almond butter

2 tablespoons mesquite powder

2 tablespoons lucuma powder

2 tablespoons hemp protein powder

½ tablespoons maca root powder

1 teaspoon coconut butter (sometimes called coconut oil)

1 teaspoon cacao butter

Pinch of sea salt

Tiny seeds of 1 vanilla bean (optional)

1 teaspoon spirulina or green powder (optional)

In a high-speed blender, combine all of the ingredients and blend until smooth.

Raw Chocolate Pudding

Serves 2

A THICK AND CREAMY coconut pudding flavored with real, raw chocolate. Finally, chocolate for breakfast—and it's healthy!

Flesh of 5 Thai coconuts

¼ cup agave nectar

3 tablespoons carob powder

2 tablespoons cacao nibs or powder

2 tablespoons mesquite or lucuma powder

1 teaspoon coconut butter (sometimes called coconut oil) or cacao butter

Tiny seeds of 1 vanilla bean (optional)

In a high-speed blender, combine all of the ingredients and blend until thick and smooth. Transfer to a bowl.

GARNISHES
Fresh strawberries, raspberries, and/or cacao nibs

FIVE

SOUPS

Soups are my specialty. I learned a lot about making them from my good friend Michael Davis, who worked as a chef for years in various restaurants around L.A. For me, creating a raw soup recipe is a bit like being a magician, pouring just the right amount of this and that into a cauldron until it's just right. Another friend took to calling me "Soup King" because she enjoyed my soups so much.

In raw cuisine, soups are made in a blender and can be prepared from scratch in just a few minutes. All the recipes I've included here have very deep and layered flavors. They are a great way to begin any meal, and are wonderful as a light meal on their own.

Dixie Chicken
Chicken-less Noodle Soup

Serves 2 to 3

A LIGHT VEGETABLE SOUP broth with diced carrots, celery, zucchini noodles, and chanterelle mushroom strips.

> 3 ½ cups daikon juice (2–3 daikon)
>
> 1 ¼ cups pure water
>
> 2 tablespoons fresh lemon juice
>
> 1 ½ teaspoons sea salt
>
> ⅛ cup diced celery
>
> ⅛ cup carrots, sliced into rounds
>
> ¼ cup zucchini, peeled and made into noodles on a Spirooli slicer
>
> ¼ cup chanterelle mushrooms

Using a juicer, juice the daikon.

In a high-speed blender, combine the daikon juice, water, lemon juice, and sea salt, and blend. Stir in the celery, carrots, and zucchini and transfer to soup bowls.

Tear the chanterelle mushrooms into thin strips and sprinkle atop the soup.

Glass Onion
French Onion Soup

Serves 2 to 3

A THIN, BRONZE-COLORED soup broth made with sweet yellow onions.

> 1 ½ cups Thai coconut water
> 1 ½ cups pure water
> ½ yellow onion, roughly chopped
> 2 cloves garlic, peeled
> ½ cup fresh lemon juice
> ¼ cup olive oil
> ¼ cup Nama Shoyu

In a high-speed blender, combine all of the ingredients and blend until smooth. Pour into a serving bowl. Using a ladle, remove and discard any foam that rises to the top.

Green River
Cucumber Watercress Soup

Serves 2 to 3

A LIGHT CUCUMBER BROTH with fresh lemon and watercress.

> 3 ½ cups cucumber juice (4–6 cucumbers)
> ⅓ cup fresh lemon juice
> ½ bunch fresh watercress
> 3 cloves garlic, peeled
> 2 tablespoons olive oil
> 2 teaspoons sea salt

Using a juicer, juice the cucumbers. In a high-speed blender, combine all of the ingredients and blend until smooth.

Harvest Corn Chowder

Serves 2 to 3

FRESH FIELD CORN creamed with pine nuts and walnuts, with a hint of fresh ground cumin.

> 1 ½ cups Thai coconut water
>
> 2 cups fresh corn, cut from the cob
>
> ½ cup raw pine nuts
>
> ½ cup raw walnuts
>
> 2 to 3 cloves garlic, peeled
>
> ¼ cup fresh lemon juice
>
> ¼ cup Nama Shoyu
>
> ½ teaspoon ground cumin

In a high-speed blender, combine all of the ingredients and blend until smooth. Pour into a serving bowl. Using a ladle, remove and discard any foam that rises to the top.

GARNISH:
Fresh corn kernels, cut from the cob

Little Green
Cream of Celery Soup

Serves 2 to 3

A LIGHT ORGANIC celery broth infused with almond cream.

    2 cups almond milk (see Note)

    2 cups celery juice from 1 bunch celery

    2 cloves garlic, peeled

    ¼ cup fresh lemon juice

    2 teaspoons sea salt

Using a juicer, juice the celery.

In a high-speed blender, combine all of the ingredients and blend until smooth. Pour into a serving bowl. Using a ladle, remove and discard any foam that rises to the top.

GARNISH:
Chopped celery

Note: To make almond milk, combine 1 cup of almonds and 3½ cups of pure water in a blender, blend until smooth, and strain through a nut-milk bag.

Mycology Cream of Shiitake Soup

Serves 2 to 3

A THICK BLEND of shiitake mushrooms and fresh vegetables creamed with almond milk.

> 3 cups almond milk (see Note)
> 2 cups shiitake mushroom caps, plus a few caps for garnish
> 3 stalks celery
> 4 cloves garlic, peeled
> ⅓ cup fresh lemon juice
> ¼ cup olive oil
> 1 ½ teaspoons sea salt

Combine all of the ingredients and blend until smooth. Pour into a serving bowl. Using a ladle, remove and discard any foam that rises to the top. Garnish with the mushroom (see below).

GARNISH:
Thinly sliced shiitake mushrooms marinated for approximately 1 minute in Nama Shoyu.

Note: To make almond milk, combine 1 cup of almonds with 3 ½ cups of pure water in a blender, blend until smooth, and strain through a nut-milk bag.

Octopus's Garden
Seaweed Chowder

Serves 2 to 3

A LIGHT YET CREAMY pine nut–based chowder, topped with soaked wakame seaweed.

- 1 ounce wakame
- 5 cups pure water
- 1 cup raw pine nuts
- 3 cloves garlic, peeled
- ¼ cup fresh lemon juice
- ½ tablespoon sea salt

Soak the seaweed in the water in a large bowl for 10 to 15 minutes. Using a strainer, strain the seaweed over another bowl. Measure 3 cups of seaweed water and discard or drink the rest. Set aside the seaweed for a garnish.

In a high-speed blender, combine the 3 cups of seaweed water with the remaining ingredients and blend until smooth. Pour into a serving bowl. Using a ladle, remove and discard any foam that rises to the top. Garnish with the seaweed.

Red Rose Speedway
Tomato Basil Soup

Serves 2 to 3

A THICK, tomato-based soup seasoned with garden-fresh basil.

    1 ½ cups Thai coconut water
    3 cups blended tomato (4–5 medium tomatoes)
    1 stalk celery
    ¼ yellow onion
    1 cup fresh basil
    5 cloves garlic, peeled
    ¼ cup fresh lemon juice
    ¼ cup olive oil
    ¼ cup Nama Shoyu
    1 teaspoon sea salt

In a high-speed blender, combine all of the ingredients and blend until smooth.

VARIATIONS:

Replace the basil with an equal amount of fresh cilantro, dill, mint, oregano, or tarragon—or experiment and find a tasty combination of herbs.

Scarborough Fair
Vegetable Soup

Serves 2 to 3

A TRADITIONAL vegetable soup flavored with parsley, sage, rosemary, and thyme.

¾ cup Thai coconut water

¾ cup pure water

2 stalks celery

¼ yellow onion

1 cucumber, peeled

1 carrot, peeled

¼ red bell pepper, seeded

5 to 6 fresh sage leaves

3 cloves garlic, peeled

2 tablespoon fresh lemon juice

¼ cup olive oil

1 teaspoon sea salt

Chopped parsley to taste

Minced rosemary leaves to taste

Minced thyme to taste

In a high-speed blender, combine all of the ingredients and blend until smooth. Pour into a serving bowl. Using a ladle, remove and discard any foam that rises to the top.

GARNISHES

Chopped carrots

Chopped celery

Chopped yellow onion

Siamese Dream
Thai Curry Soup

Serves 2 to 3

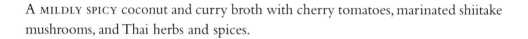

A MILDLY SPICY coconut and curry broth with cherry tomatoes, marinated shiitake mushrooms, and Thai herbs and spices.

3 cups Thai coconut water

3 cloves garlic, peeled

One 2-inch piece ginger, peeled

¼ cup fresh lemon juice

¼ cup olive oil

¼ cup Nama Shoyu

1 tablespoon curry powder

In a high-speed blender, combine all of the ingredients and blend until smooth. Pour into a serving bowl. Using a ladle, remove and discard any foam that rises to the top. The soup broth is amazing on its own, but adding any or all of the following garnishes takes it to the next level.

GARNISHES

Chopped avocado

Minced chives

Sliced cherry tomatoes

Chopped red bell pepper

Chopped basil leaves

Chopped mint leaves

Chopped cilantro

Sliced shiitake mushrooms, marinated for approximately 1 minute in Nama Shoyu

Thick 'N' Thin
Sprouted Lentil Chili

Serves 2 to 3

A THICK, fresh vegetable-and-tomato chili topped with sprouted lentils.

> 2 cups blended tomato (3–4 medium tomatoes)
> ½ cucumber, peeled
> 2 stalks celery
> ½ red bell pepper, seeded
> 1 cup fresh basil, mint, or cilantro leaves, or a combination
> ½ cup whole-leaf dulse
> 3 cloves garlic, peeled
> ⅓ cup fresh lemon juice
> ¼ cup olive oil
> ¼ cup Nama Shoyu
> 1 ½ tablespoons chili powder
> 1 teaspoon ground cumin
> ½ teaspoon sea salt

In a high-speed blender, combine all of the ingredients and blend until smooth.

GARNISHES
Sprouted red or green lentils (available at health food stores)
Chopped celery
Chopped red bell pepper
Chopped scallions

Ruby Tuesday Borscht

Serves 2 to 3

A BRILLIANT CRIMSON BLEND of beet juice, garden vegetables, and fresh dill.

    1 cup beet juice (2–3 bunches)
    1 cup carrot juice (4–6 carrots)
    1 cup celery juice (5–6 stalks)
    ¼ cup fresh lemon juice
    1 to 2 cloves garlic
    1 ½ teaspoons sea salt
    ½ bunch fresh dill

Using a juicer, separately juice the beets, carrots, and celery. In a high-speed blender, combine all of the ingredients and blend until smooth.

SIX

DRESSINGS
& Sauces

This section contains salad dressings as well as sauces to accompany other dishes in this book. A salad, after all, is only as good as its dressing. These dressings, made in a blender, will inspire you to eat more greens. Whether you're having mescaline, a spring mix, or a hearty blend of kale, collards, and chard, these dressings will take your salad to the next level. I am notorious for using lots of dressing—so much so that my salads sometimes resemble thick soups. You, however, can use as much or as little dressing as you like. Unless otherwise noted, these dressing are to be served over your favorite salad greens.

Mushroom Gravy

Makes about 3 cups

A MUSHROOM, vegetable, and tahini gravy with a traditional flavor.

⅓ cup Thai coconut water

⅓ cup pure water

1 ½ cups portobello or white mushrooms

¼ cup tahini

4 cloves garlic, peeled

2 tablespoons fresh lemon juice

2 tablespoons Nama Shoyu

½ stalk celery

¼ carrot

2 tablespoons chopped yellow onion

¼ red bell pepper

¾ teaspoon sea salt

In a high-speed blender, combine all of the ingredients and blend until smooth.

SERVING SUGGESTION: Serve with the Mashed "Potatoes" (page 115).

BBQ Sauce with Nut Loaf

BBQ Sauce

ALL THE ELEMENTS of the best BBQ sauce, but made with the finest raw, organic ingredients.

1 ½ cups blended tomato
   (2–3 medium tomatoes)
¼ cup raw apple cider vinegar
2 tablespoons Nama Shoyu
2 tablespoons agave nectar

2 tablespoons chopped yellow onion
4 cloves garlic, peeled
1 cup sun-dried tomatoes
1 tablespoon chili powder

In a high-speed blender, combine all of the ingredients and blend until smooth.

SERVING SUGGESTION: Serve with Nut Loaf (page 155).

Creamy Ranch Dressing

Makes about 2 cups

SIMILAR TO the ranch dressing you get at the grocery store, except it won't kill you.

¾ cup Thai coconut water
2 to 3 cloves garlic, peeled
⅓ cup fresh lemon juice

½ teaspoon sea salt
1 cup raw macadamia nuts, pine nuts, or
   cashews, or a combination of the three

In a high-speed blender, combine all of the ingredients and blend until smooth.

Apple-Ginger Dressing

Makes about 2½ cups

SWEET APPLE JUICE spiced with fresh ginger root and thickened with raw tahini.

1¼ cup fresh apple juice (4–6 cored apples)
¼ cup fresh lemon juice
¼ cup raw tahini
2 tablespoons olive oil

2 tablespoons Nama Shoyu
2 tablespoons agave nectar
2 to 3 cloves garlic, peeled
One 2-inch piece ginger, peeled

Using a juicer, juice the apples. In a high-speed blender, combine all of the ingredients and blend until smooth. Pour into a serving bowl. Using a ladle, remove and discard any foam that rises to the top.

Citrus-Hemp Dressing

Makes about 2¾ cups

Tangy orange and lemon juice blended with the nutty flavor of raw hemp seeds.

1¼ cup fresh orange juice
¼ cup fresh lemon juice
¼ cup Nama Shoyu
¼ cup olive oil
2 tablespoons raw apple cider vinegar

½ cup hemp seeds
2 to 3 cloves garlic, peeled
One 2-inch piece ginger, peeled
½ teaspoon sea salt

In a high-speed blender, combine all of the ingredients and blend until smooth. Pour into a serving bowl. Using a ladle, remove and discard any foam that rises to the top.

Creamy Italian Dressing

Makes about 2 cups

A CREAMY oil-and-vinegar dressing infused with fresh basil and oregano.

¾ cup olive oil

¼ cup raw apple cider vinegar

2 to 3 cloves garlic, peeled

2 tablespoons fresh lemon juice

1 ½ teaspoons sea salt

½ cup fresh basil leaves

¼ cup fresh oregano leaves

⅓ cup pure water

⅓ cup raw pine nuts

In a high-speed blender, combine all of the ingredients and blend until smooth. Pour into a serving bowl. Using a ladle, remove and discard any foam that rises to the top.

VARIATION:
For a lighter version, omit the water and pine nuts.

Cocktail Sauce

Makes about 3 ½ cups

HORSERADISH ROOT pureed in fresh and sun-dried tomatoes.

2 cups blended tomato

2 tablespoons fresh lemon juice

2 tablespoons agave nectar

2 to 3 cloves garlic, peeled

½ to 1 cup sun-dried tomatoes

½ cup peeled horseradish root, chopped

1 teaspoon sea salt

In a high-speed blender, combine all of the ingredients and blend until smooth.

SERVING SUGGESTION: Serve with Veggie Cakes (page 154).

Garlic Cream Dressing

Makes about 2 cups

A SIMPLE, yet rich and amazing, emulsified dressing made from only five ingredients.

¼ cup fresh lemon juice

¼ cup Nama Shoyu

8 cloves garlic, peeled

One 3-inch piece ginger, peeled

1 ¼ cups olive oil

In a high-speed blender, combine the lemon juice, Nama Shoyu, garlic, and ginger. While the blender is running, add the olive oil slowly in a stream until the dressing thickens and emulsifies (you may not use the full 1 ¼ cups of oil).

Ketchup
Makes about 2 ½ cups

I USED TO WORK in the same town where a well-known brand of ketchup is made. It smelled so rank, I vowed never to eat ketchup again. Then I came up with this amazing recipe.

 ¾ cup blended tomato (1–2 medium tomatoes)
 ¼ cup raw apple cider vinegar
 2 tablespoons Nama Shoyu
 2 tablespoons agave nectar
 2 to 3 cloves garlic, peeled
 1 to 1 ½ cups sun-dried tomatoes

In a high-speed blender, combine all of the ingredients and blend until smooth.

SERVING SUGGESTION: Serve with the Big Matt with Cheese (page 125).

Dressings & Sauces

Marinara Sauce with Cheese Sticks

Marinara or Pizza Sauce

Makes about 3 cups

THE SAVORY sun-dried tomato sauce that appears in several recipes, including all of the pizzas.

> 1 ½ cups blended tomato (2–3 medium tomatoes)
> ½ cup fresh lemon juice
> 2 tablespoons Nama Shoyu
> 2 tablespoons olive oil
> 2 tablespoons chopped yellow onion
> 3 cloves garlic, peeled
> 1 cup sun-dried tomatoes
> Pinch of sea salt

In a high-speed blender, combine all of the ingredients and blend until smooth.

SERVING SUGGESTIONS: Serve with Zucchini Pasta Marinara (page 132) or Cheese Sticks (page 84).

Mayonnaise

A CREAMY MAYO that you'll feel great about eating.

1 ½ cups Thai coconut water

5 cloves garlic, peeled

¾ cup fresh lemon juice

2 teaspoons sea salt

½ cup stone-ground mustard

2 cups raw macadamia nuts, pine nuts, or cashews, or any combination of the three

In a high-speed blender, combine all of the ingredients and blend until smooth.

SERVING SUGGESTION: Serve with the Mock Tuna Salad (page 126).

Mint-Tahini Sauce

Makes about 2 cups

A SUPER-THICK and super-minty tahini sauce that goes great with my Falafel.

¾ cup fresh lemon juice

¼ cup olive oil

¼ cup Nama Shoyu

2 to 3 cloves garlic, peeled

1 cup raw tahini

1 bunch fresh mint leaves, stems removed

In a high-speed blender, combine all of the ingredients and blend until smooth.

SERVING SUGGESTION: Serve with Falafel (page 140).

Sun-Dried Tomato Dressing

Makes about 2 cups

The FLAVOR of sun-dried tomatoes concentrated in a tasty salad dressing.

½ cup olive oil

½ cup raw apple cider vinegar

½ cup Nama Shoyu

¼ cup fresh lemon juice

3 cloves garlic, peeled

⅓ to ½ cup sun-dried tomatoes

In a high-speed blender, combine all of the ingredients and blend until smooth.

Sweet Herb Oil Dressing

Makes about 2 cups

This DRESSING is so good that I sometimes serve it as a soup!

¾ cup Thai coconut water

2 to 3 cloves garlic, peeled

¼ cup fresh lemon juice

½ cup olive oil

2 tablespoons Nama Shoyu

2 tablespoons agave nectar

Pinch of sea salt

1 cup fresh basil, mint, cilantro, dill, or tarragon, or any combination of the five

In a high-speed blender, combine all of the ingredients and blend until smooth. Pour into a serving bowl. Using a ladle, remove and discard any foam that rises to the top.

Creamy Dill Sauce

Makes about 2 cups

FRESH DILL WEED in a creamy, nut-based salad dressing.

¾ cup Thai coconut water

2 to 3 cloves garlic, peeled

⅓ cup fresh lemon juice

½ teaspoon sea salt

1 cup raw macadamia nuts, pine nuts, or cashews, or a combination of the three

1 bunch dill with stems

In a high-speed blender, combine all of the ingredients and blend until smooth.

SERVING SUGGESTION: Serve with the Veggie Cakes (page 154).

Creamy Dill Sauce with Veggie Cakes

SEVEN

APPETIZERS &
Side Dishes

My hummus will take the Pepsi challenge against cooked hummus any day of the week! In fact, if you were to bring any one of the dishes in this chapter to your next social gathering, most people would not even *realize* it's raw, and it will be the talk of the buffet table! These dishes are the main items we serve at our café in Santa Monica. Try your hand at making them and come in to taste mine when you're in the neighborhood.

●   ●   ●

Cauliflower Couscous

Serves 3 to 4

FINELY GROUND CAULIFLOWER SALAD with Greek olives and Mediterranean herbs.

2 heads cauliflower, finely ground
   in a food processor

½ fresh cup lemon juice

1 cup olive oil

1 tablespoon plus 1 teaspoon black pepper

¾ teaspoon sea salt

1 bunch fresh parsley, stems removed

1 bunch fresh mint, stems removed

1 bunch fresh cilantro, stems removed

One 13-ounce jar pitted Greek olives

In a large mixing bowl, combine all of the ingredients and mix thoroughly.

Marinated Bok Choy Salad

Serves 4

TENDER baby bok choy lightly marinated in raw soy sauce, garlic, and olive oil.

5 heads baby bok choy

⅓ cup olive oil

¼ cup Nama Shoyu

4 cloves garlic, peeled

Starting from the bottom of the plant, chop the bok choy stalks into half-inch pieces, leaving the leaves whole. In a blender, combine the olive oil, Nama Shoyu, and garlic and blend thoroughly. Add to the bok choy, mix well, and serve.

Cheese Sticks

Serves 3 to 4

A SAVORY, dehydrated appetizer that even kids love.

> 4 ¾ cups raw sunflower seeds
> ½ cup fresh lemon juice
> ½ cup Nama Shoyu
> 4 cloves garlic, peeled

Grind 2 ¾ cups of the sunflower seeds in a food processor.

Spread out 2 cups of the ground seeds on a large plate.

In a high-speed blender, combine the lemon juice, Nama Shoyu, garlic, and the remaining 2 ¾ cups of whole sunflower seeds, and blend until smooth. Transfer the resulting mixture to a pastry bag, then use the bag to squeeze out the dough onto the plate of finely ground sunflower seeds into sticks that are approximately 3 ¾ inches long. Gently roll the sticks in the ground sunflower seeds until they are evenly covered on all sides.

Carefully transfer the sticks to a dehydrator sheet. Dehydrate at 100°F for 18 to 24 hours. Serve while still warm, with Marinara Sauce (page 73).

Sunflower Seed Cheese

Serves 4

A THICK, SPREADABLE CHEESE that is as versatile as it is tasty.

½ cup fresh lemon juice

½ cup Nama Shoyu

4 to 5 cloves garlic, peeled

2 ¾ cups raw sunflower seeds,
    very finely ground in a food processor

In a high-speed blender, combine all of the ingredients, adding the sunflower seeds last. Blend thoroughly until the resulting cheese is smooth and uniform.

SERVING SUGGESTIONS: Spread this cheese on RAWvolution's Famous Onion Bread (page 100), or on sliced cucumbers, celery, and carrot sticks.

Summer Corn Salad

Serves 3 to 4

KERNELS OF FRESH SWEET CORN cut from the cob and tossed with diced celery and scallions in a creamy sauce.

FOR THE SALAD:

3 cups fresh corn kernels, cut from the cob (approximately 4 ears)

1 cup roughly chopped celery

1 cup chopped scallions

1 bunch fresh cilantro, stems removed

FOR THE DRESSING:

½ cup Thai coconut water

¼ cup fresh lemon juice

2 tablespoons agave nectar

2 tablespoons olive oil

1 ½ teaspoons sea salt

1 tablespoon curry powder

¼ cup raw pine nuts

In a large mixing bowl, combine all of the salad ingredients and toss to mix thoroughly.

In a high-speed blender, combine all of the dressing ingredients and blend until smooth. Pour over the salad, toss well to mix the dressing with the corn, and serve.

Creamy Cabbage Coleslaw

Serves 3 to 4

Two TYPES of finely shredded cabbage, tossed with shredded carrots and red radish, in a thick garlic cream dressing.

FOR THE SALAD:

½ cup peeled and shredded carrots

½ cup shredded radish

2 cups finely shredded green cabbage

2 cups finely shredded red cabbage

FOR THE DRESSING:

2 tablespoons raw apple cider vinegar

2 tablespoons Nama Shoyu

4 cloves garlic, peeled

One 2-inch piece ginger, peeled

Approximately 1 ¼ cups olive oil

In a large mixing bowl, combine all of the salad ingredients and toss to mix thoroughly.

To make the dressing, in a high-speed blender, combine the vinegar, Nama Shoyu, garlic, and ginger. While the blender is running, add the olive oil gradually in a steady stream until the dressing thickens and emulsifies (you may not need the full 1 ¼ cups). Pour the dressing over the salad, mix well, and serve.

Cucumber-Dill Salad

Serves 3 to 4

THINLY SLICED FIELD CUCUMBERS, diced red onions, and fresh dill in a tangy lemon dressing.

FOR THE SALAD:

    5 cucumbers, peeled and thinly sliced

    1 red onion, diced

    2 bunches chopped dill, stems removed

FOR THE DRESSING:

    ½ cup raw apple cider vinegar

    ½ cup olive oil

    ½ cup fresh lemon juice

    1 tablespoon sea salt

    5 cloves garlic, peeled

In a large mixing bowl, combine all of the salad ingredients and toss to mix thoroughly.

In a high-speed blender, combine the dressing ingredients and blend until smooth. Pour the dressing over the salad, mix well, and serve.

Egg-less Egg Salad

Serves 3 to 4

A VIBRANT-YELLOW macadamia cream salad with diced celery, scallions, and red bell peppers.

> ½ cup pure water
> ½ cup fresh lemon juice
> 1 ½ teaspoons turmeric
> 2 cloves garlic, peeled
> 1 ½ teaspoons sea salt
> 1 ½ cups raw macadamia nuts or cashews
> ⅓ cup chopped scallions
> ⅓ cup chopped celery
> ⅓ cup chopped red bell pepper

In a high-speed blender, combine the water, lemon juice, turmeric, garlic, sea salt, and nuts and blend until smooth.

In a medium mixing bowl, combine the contents of the blender with the scallions, celery, and bell peppers. Mix well and serve.

Going to California
Guacamole

Serves 2 to 3

1

CREAMY, RIPE AVOCADO with tomato, scallions, and cilantro. Like traditional guac—but fresher!

  3 medium avocados
  1 cup chopped scallions
  1 bunch cilantro, stems removed
  1 cup chopped tomatoes
  ¼ cup fresh lemon juice
  1 teaspoon sea salt
  3 to 4 cloves garlic, peeled
  2 tablespoons olive oil

Combine all of the ingredients in a mixing bowl, mix well, and serve.

SERVING SUGGESTIONS: Serve with RAWvolution's Famous Onion Bread (page 100), or on Soft Tacos (page 145), or a Tostada (page 156).

Appetizers & Side Dishes

Maggie's Farm
Marinated Greens

Serves 4

1 ◎

I GET MY BABY GREENS from an amazing grower north of Los Angeles called Maggie's Farm. Maggie's Farm is fantastic! Not only are they named after a great Bob Dylan song, they also have the finest greens I've ever tasted.

FOR THE SALAD:
>   12 loosely packed cups (total) whole baby spinach leaves,
>   baby kale leaves, tatsoi leaves, mizuna leaves, baby romaine leaves,
>   or baby chard leaves, in any combination

FOR THE DRESSING:
>   ½ cup fresh lemon juice
>   ½ cup Nama Shoyu
>   ½ cup olive oil
>   3 to 4 cloves garlic, peeled
>   ½ cup stone-ground mustard
>   1 tablespoon ground cumin

In a large mixing bowl, combine all of the salad greens and mix thoroughly.

In a high-speed blender, combine all of the dressing ingredients and blend until smooth. Pour over the salad, toss to mix well, and serve.

Mediterranean Tabouli

Serves 3 to 4

A FRESH PARSLEY SALAD with cherry tomatoes, chopped yellow onions, and hemp seeds in a creamy lemon dressing.

FOR THE SALAD:

> 6 bunches fresh parsley
>
> 1 cup chopped cherry tomatoes
>
> ½ cup hemp seeds
>
> ½ cup chopped yellow onion

FOR THE DRESSING:

> ½ cup fresh lemon juice
>
> ½ cup olive oil
>
> ½ teaspoon sea salt
>
> 5 cloves garlic, peeled

To make the salad, in a food processor, chop the parsley with the metal "S" blade. Transfer to a large mixing bowl and add the tomato, hemp seeds, and yellow onion. Mix the ingredients together thoroughly with a spatula or wooden spoon.

In a high-speed blender, combine all of the dressing ingredients and blend until smooth. Pour over the salad, toss to mix well, and serve.

RAWvolution's
Famous Onion Bread

Makes 9 servings

A DELICIOUS, soft flat bread that you won't believe is made with only five ingredients.

3 large yellow onions

¾ cups flax seed, ground in a high speed blender

¾ cups raw sunflower seeds, ground in a food processor

½ cup Nama Shoyu

⅓ cups olive oil

Peel and halve the onions. In a food processor, cut the onions with the slicing disc. Transfer the cut onions to a large mixing bowl, add the remaining ingredients, and mix until the ingredients are thoroughly combined.

Spread 2 cups of the mixture evenly on a dehydrator tray pined with a Teflex sheet. Repeat until all of the mixture is used. Dehydrate at 100°F for 24 hours. Flip the tray over onto a work surface, and gently peel the Teflex sheet off the bread. Return to the dehydrator for another 12 hours. Once dehydrated, cut into 9 equal pieces (make 2 cuts horizontally and 2 cuts vertically).

SERVING SUGGESTIONS: Serve alone or as an accompaniment to any soup, salad, or side dish. Or use to make any of the sandwiches and pizza crusts in this book.

Fresh Tomato Salsa

Serves 3 to 4

EVERYTHING a great salsa should have, including enzymes!

2 cups chopped tomatoes

¾ cup chopped fresh cilantro

½ cup chopped yellow onions or scallions

2 tablespoons fresh lemon or lime juice

1 tablespoon olive oil

4 cloves garlic, minced

Rounded ¼ teaspoon cayenne pepper

¾ teaspoon sea salt

1 ½ teaspoons ground cumin

¾ teaspoon ground coriander

Combine all of the ingredients in a medium mixing bowl, mix well, and serve.

SERVING SUGGESTIONS: Serve with Soft Taco (page 145) or Tostada (page 156).

No-Bean Hummus

Serves 3 to 4

A THICK, bean-less raw hummus made with zucchini and raw sesame tahini.

2 zucchini, peeled and chopped

¾ cup raw tahini

½ cup fresh lemon juice

¼ cup olive oil

4 cloves garlic, peeled

2 ½ teaspoons sea salt

½ tablespoon ground cumin

In a high-speed blender, combine all of the ingredients and blend until thick and smooth.

SERVING SUGGESTION: Serve with RAWvolution's Famous Onion Bread (page 100), slices of cucumber or zucchini, celery stalks, or carrot sticks.

Savory Herb Stuffing

Serves 3 to 4

A WELL-SEASONED BLEND of nuts and seeds, fresh vegetables, herbs, and marinated mushrooms.

1 cup soaked raw walnuts (see Note),
   finely ground in a food processor

1 cup soaked raw pumpkin seeds (see Note),
   finely ground in a food processor

1 cup soaked raw sunflower seeds (see Note),
   finely ground in a food processor

⅓ cup chopped yellow onion

¾ cup diced celery

1 cup chopped mushrooms, briefly marinated
   in 1 or 2 tablespoons Nama Shoyu

2 tablespoons olive oil

¼ teaspoon sea salt

½ teaspoon black pepper

1 ½ teaspoons kelp

1 ½ teaspoons sage

1 ½ teaspoons thyme

In a mixing bowl, combine all of the ingredients, mix well, and serve.

Note: Soak the nuts and seeds in pure water for 2 to 4 hours; then drain and dry.

Tapenade-Stuffed
Shiitake Mushroom Caps
Makes about 60 mushrooms

BABY SHIITAKE MUSHROOM CAPS stuffed with a rich pine nut, Italian olive, and herb tapenade.

> 2 cups chopped Italian olives
>
> 1 cup raw pine nuts, ground in a food processor
>
> 5 cloves garlic, minced
>
> ¼ cup stone-ground mustard
>
> 1 cup minced fresh basil, chives, cilantro, dill, and tarragon, in any combination.
>
> Approximately 60 shiitake mushrooms, stems removed

In a medium mixing bowl, combine the olives, pine nuts, garlic, mustard, and herbs and mix thoroughly. Using a small spoon, spread enough of the mixture on the underside of each mushroom cap to completely cover. Place on a dehydrator tray and dehydrate at 100°F for 12 to 18 hours.

Thai Coleslaw

Serves 3 to 4

ONE DAY MY MOM CALLED me and said she found a Thai coleslaw recipe in a magazine that she thought I could re-create in a raw version. It was pretty simple; I just replaced some of the ingredients in the dressing with better quality ones and added some fresh Thai herbs.

FOR THE SALAD:

3 cups finely shredded green or
   Napa cabbage

1 cup peeled and shredded zucchini

1 cup shredded carrot

1 bunch fresh basil, stems removed
   and leaves chopped

1 bunch mint, stems removed and
   leaves chopped

1 bunch fresh cilantro, stems removed
   and leaves chopped

1 bunch fresh chives, chopped

½ cup raw, unsalted peanuts

FOR THE DRESSING:

2 tablespoons fresh lemon juice

2 tablespoons apple cider vinegar

¼ cup Nama Shoyu

2 tablespoons agave nectar

¼ cup olive oil

2 cloves garlic, peeled

One 1-inch piece ginger, peeled

1 teaspoon chili powder

1 ½ tablespoons curry powder

In a large mixing bowl, combine all of the salad ingredients and toss to mix thoroughly.

In a high-speed blender, combine all of the dressing ingredients and blend until smooth. Pour the dressing over the salad, mix well, and serve.

Nopalito
Cactus Salad

Serves 3 to 4

A COLORFUL and healthful mix of Nopalito cactus, sweet corn from the cob, and shredded red cabbage.

FOR THE SALAD:

    1 ½ cups Nopalito cactus, spines removed and
        flesh cut into small cubes

    1 cup corn kernels, cut from the cob (about 2 ears)

    ½ cup chopped celery

    ½ cup chopped scallions

    ½ cup finely shredded red cabbage

FOR THE DRESSING:

    ⅓ cup fresh lemon juice

    ⅓ cup olive oil

    1 ½ teaspoons sea salt

    ¼ teaspoon cayenne pepper

In a large mixing bowl, combine all of the salad ingredients and toss to mix thoroughly.

In a high-speed blender, combine all of the dressing ingredients and blend until smooth. Pour the dressing over the salad, mix well, and serve.

Mashed "Potatoes"

Mashed "Potatoes"

Serves 3 to 4

FLUFFY CAULIFLOWER and macadamia nut "potatoes," topped with freshly ground pepper.

2 ½ cups cauliflower,
    ground in a food processor

¼ cup raw macadamia nuts,
    ground in a food processor

¼ cup olive oil

1 teaspoon sea salt

1 very small clove garlic, peeled

Freshly ground black pepper to taste

In a food processor, combine all of the ingredients except the pepper and process until the mixture looks fluffy, like conventional mashed potatoes. Top with freshly ground pepper.

Broccolini Salad

Serves 3

FRESH YOUNG broccoli stalks and florets in a simple sea salt and olive oil marinade.

3 broccolini (baby broccoli) or regular broccoli bunches
⅓ cup olive oil
3 ¾ teaspoons sea salt

Cut the florets off of the broccolini stalks. Transfer the stalks to a food processor, and process with the shredding disc. In a large mixing bowl, combine the shredded stalks, the florets, olive oil, and sea salt and mix thoroughly.

Mango Chutney

Serves 2 to 3

SOME FOLKS BELIEVE chutney should be so spicy that you can't eat it, and so sweet that you can't stop. This version is only mildly spiced, but feel free to double the amount of cayenne.

 2 cups chopped mango

 2 tablespoons fresh lemon juice

 1 ½ teaspoons raw apple cider vinegar

 2 tablespoons stone-ground mustard

 ¼ teaspoon sea salt

 2 cloves garlic, peeled and crushed with a garlic press

 1 ½ teaspoons agave nectar

 1 bunch chopped fresh cilantro

 ¼ cup finely chopped red bell pepper

 ¼ cup finely chopped red onion or scallions

 ¼ teaspoon cayenne pepper

In a mixing bowl, combine all of the ingredients, mix well, and serve.

SERVING SUGGESTIONS: Serve with Falafel (page 140).

Cheese Pierogies

Serves 3 to 4

HALF-MOON SHAPED bites of rich cashew cheese in a delicate jicama shell.

FOR THE CASHEW CHEESE FILLING:

¼ cup fresh lemon juice

¼ cup Nama Shoyu

¼ red bell pepper

2 to 3 cloves garlic, peeled

1 to 1 ½ cups raw cashews, macadamia nuts,
pine nuts, or a combination

FOR THE PIEROGIE SHELL:

1 small jicama, peeled and sliced very thinly into
rounds with a mandoline slicer.

In a high-speed blender, combine all of the filling ingredients and blend until the resulting cashew cheese in uniform and smooth. Using a spoon, place a small dollop of the cashew cheese in the center of one of the jicama slices. Fold the jicama in half, creating a half-moon shape. The edges of the jicama should stick together and create a seal. Repeat until all the jicama and cheese are used.

EIGHT

ENTREES

love the challenge of creating dishes like pizza, pasta, and sandwiches from raw fruits and vegetables! It is so great to sit down to something as substantial as a sandwich or a nice fat wrap. At a dinner I once catered, a gentleman who had never eaten prepared raw food before remarked, "When I heard this was a raw food dinner, I thought you were serving radishes and stuff; then you go and break out a lasagna!" I liked that.

Sloppy Joe Sandwich

Serves 2

DEHYDRATED nut and veggie pâté in a rich, sun-dried tomato marinara, layered over crisp lettuce and served between two pieces of my Famous Onion Bread.

¼ tray crumbled Nut Loaf (page 155)

½ recipe Marinara Sauce (page 73)

1 tablespoon chili powder

2 teaspoons raw apple cider vinegar

1 tablespoon mesquite powder

Four 4¾-inch square pieces RAWvolution's Famous
   Onion Bread (page 100), each cut diagonally into 2 triangles

2 cups shredded lettuce

In a mixing bowl, combine all of the ingredients except the Onion Bread and lettuce, and mix thoroughly. Place a quarter of the shredded lettuce on an Onion Bread triangle, then scoop roughly a quarter of the nut loaf mixture and lay on top of the lettuce. Top with a second triangle to make a sandwich. Repeat with the remaining ingredients until all the Nut Loaf and Onion Bread has been used.

Big Matt
with Cheese

Serves 1

PEOPLE ARE OFTEN SURPRISED to learn that I worked at McDonald's while in high school. Here's *my* no-beef patty, special sauce, lettuce, cheese, pickles, and onions on a sunflower seed bun.

1 ½ teaspoons of Ketchup (page 71)

One 4 ¾-inch square piece RAWvolution's Famous
   Onion Bread (page 100) cut diagonally into 2 triangles

2 to 3 leaves lettuce of your choice

1 thin slice yellow onion

1 tablespoon Sunflower Seed Cheese (page 85)

1 nut loaf burger patty (see Variation, page 155)

5 to 6 slices raw, organic pickles

2 thick tomato slices

½ tablespoon stone-ground mustard

Spread the Ketchup on an Onion Bread round. Stack the remaining ingredients, except the mustard, on top. Spread the mustard on the second Onion Bread triangle, set atop the Big Matt, and serve.

Mock Tuna Salad

Serves 4

A HEARTY SUNFLOWER PÂTÉ with diced celery, scallions, dried dill, and dulse in a creamy, nut-based mayo.

FOR THE SALAD:

3 cups soaked raw sunflower seeds (see Note), ground in a food processor

3 to 4 stalks celery, diced

½ bunch scallions, diced

2 tablespoons dulse flakes

¼ cup dried dill

FOR THE DRESSING:

1 ½ cups Thai coconut water

6 cloves garlic, peeled

1 cup fresh lemon juice

1 tablespoon sea salt

2 ½ cups raw macadamia nuts, cashews, pine nuts, or a combination

½ cup stone-ground mustard

In a large mixing bowl, combine all of the salad ingredients and toss to mix thoroughly.

In a high-speed blender, combine all of the dressing ingredients and blend thoroughly. Pour the dressing over the salad, toss to mix well, and serve.

Note: Soak the sunflower seeds in pure water for 2 to 4 hours; drain and dry.

SERVING SUGGESTIONS: Serve as is, on a green salad, between 2 pieces of RAWvolution's Famous Onion Bread (page 100) with stone-ground mustard, or wrapped in a collard green or romaine lettuce leaf.

MOCK CHICKEN SALAD:

Replace the dulse flakes and dried dill with 2 tablespoons each of dried thyme, oregano, and sage.

Asian Vegetable Nori Rolls

Serves 4

1

AVOCADO, daikon, carrots, scallions, cucumber, red bell pepper, and clover sprouts in a raw, fish-free nori roll.

4 sheets raw nori

4 large, flat collard green or
    romaine lettuce leaves

1 ½ cups shredded carrots

1 ½ cups shredded daikon

1 avocado, thinly sliced

8 scallions (green parts only)

2 cups clover sprouts

¼ cucumber, seeded and cut lengthwise
    into 4 long, thin slices

1 red bell pepper, seeded and thinly
    sliced

Lay out the nori sheets on a clean, dry surface. Arrange a collard green or romaine leaf on top of each nori sheet so that it completely covers the half of the sheet that is closest to you. These leaves will prevent the vegetables from getting the nori sheets wet, which makes the nori more prone to tearing.

Place a narrow layer of the carrots along the length of each nori sheet, about ½ inch from the end closest to you. Top with the daikon, avocado, scallions, sprouts, cucumber, and bell peppers, keeping the ingredients in a narrow pile.

Fold the edge of the nori closest to you over the filling. Gently roll each nori away from you, tightly and evenly, into a firm, snugly wrapped roll. Seal the exposed edge of the nori to the roll by wetting it with a little pure water or Nama Shoyu.

Cut each roll into 2 pieces with a sharp, serrated knife.

Zucchini
Pasta Alfredo

Serves 3 to 4

SPAGHETTI-STYLE ZUCCHINI noodles bathed in a rich, nut-based Alfredo cream sauce with a touch of nutmeg.

- ¾ cup Thai coconut water
- 2 cloves garlic, peeled
- ⅓ cup fresh lemon juice
- 1 teaspoon sea salt
- 1 cup raw pine nuts or cashews, or a combination
- ½ teaspoon ground nutmeg
- 6 to 8 zucchini, peeled and cut like spaghetti
  with a Spirooli slicer according to the manufacturer's
  instructions (see Note)

In a high-speed blender, combine all of the ingredients except the zucchini noodles, and blend until they are smooth. Put the zucchini noodles in a serving bowl, pour the Alfredo sauce over the noodles, mix well, and serve.

Note: The texture of the zucchini noodles improves when they are left to sit in the open air at room temperature for 6 to 8 hours.

Clockwise from left: Pasta Marinara, Zucchini Pasta Alfredo, Pesto Pasta

Zucchini
Pasta Marinara

Serves 3 to 4

SPAGHETTI-STYLE zucchini noodles in a thick, sun-dried tomato marinara sauce.

1 ½ cups blended tomato

½ cup fresh lemon juice

2 tablespoons Nama Shoyu

2 tablespoons olive oil

2 tablespoons chopped yellow onion

3 cloves garlic, peeled

1 cup sun-dried tomatoes

Pinch of sea salt

6 to 8 zucchini, peeled and cut like spaghetti noodles
with a Spirooli slicer according to manufacturer's
instructions (see Note)

In a high-speed blender, combine all of the ingredients, except the zucchini noodles, and blend until they are smooth. Put the noodles in a serving bowl, pour the sauce over them, mix well, and serve.

Note: The texture of the zucchini noodles improves when they are left to sit in the open air at room temperature for 6 to 8 hours.

Pesto Pasta

Serves 3 to 4

SPAGHETTI-STYLE zucchini noodles in a creamy pine nut–and–basil pesto sauce.

¾ cup Thai coconut water

2 to 3 cloves garlic, peeled

⅓ cup fresh lemon juice

½ teaspoon sea salt

1 cup raw pine nuts

1 cup fresh basil

2 tablespoons olive oil

6 to 8 zucchini, peeled and cut like spaghetti noodles
with a Spirooli slicer according to manufacturer's
instructions (see Note)

In a high-speed blender, combine all of the ingredients, except the zucchini noodles, and blend until they are smooth. Put the zucchini noodles in a serving bowl, pour the sauce over them, mix well, and serve.

Note: The texture of the zucchini noodles improves when they are left to sit in the open air at room temperature for 6 to 8 hours.

Greek Pizza, Pineapple Pizza, and Pizza Italiano

Greek Pizza

Serves 4

A CRUST OF MY FAMOUS ONION BREAD topped generously with Sunflower Seed Cheese, Pizza Sauce, fresh oregano, red bell pepper, diced red onion, and Greek olives.

4 collard green leaves

1 recipe Sunflower Seed Cheese (page 85)

1 recipe Pizza Sauce (page 75)

Four 4¾-inch square pieces RAWvolution's Famous
   Onion Bread (page 100)

1 cup chopped fresh oregano

1 cup chopped red onions

1 cup chopped red bell peppers

1 cup sun-dried tomatoes

1 cup pitted and chopped Greek olives

Cut the collard green leaves into 4 squares the same size as the bread.

Combine the Seed Cheese and Pizza Sauce in a small mixing bowl. Spread the mixture on the collard green squares, and place these on top of the Onion Bread squares. Sprinkle one fourth of the oregano over each square, covering it evenly. Repeat with the red onions, bell peppers, sun-dried tomatoes, and olives. For a more authentic pizza slice, cut into triangles to serve.

Pineapple Pizza

Serves 4

A CRUST OF MY FAMOUS ONION BREAD topped generously with Sunflower Seed Cheese, Pizza Sauce, fresh basil, diced red onion, red bell pepper, and chunks of fresh pineapple.

    4 collard green leaves
    1 recipe Sunflower Seed Cheese (page 85)
    1 recipe Pizza Sauce (page 75)
    Four 4 ¾-inches square pieces of RAWvolution's Famous
        Onion Bread (page 100)
    1 cup chopped fresh basil
    1 cup chopped red onions
    1 cup chopped red bell peppers
    1 cup chopped fresh pineapple
    ¼ cup fresh tarragon leaves

Cut the collard green leaves into 4 squares the same size as the bread.

Combine the Seed Cheese and Pizza Sauce in a small mixing bowl. Spread the mixture on the collard green squares, and place these on top of the Onion Bread squares. Sprinkle a fourth of the basil over each square, covering it evenly. Repeat with the red onions, bell peppers, pineapple, and tarragon.

Pizza Italiano

Serves 4

2

A CRUST OF MY FAMOUS ONION BREAD generously topped with sunflower seed cheese, sun-dried tomato marinara, fresh basil, oregano, red bell pepper, diced yellow onion, marinated mushrooms, and Italian olives.

> 4 collard green leaves
> 1 recipe of Sunflower Seed Cheese (page 85)
> 1 recipe of Pizza Sauce (page 75)
> Four 4 ¾-inch square pieces RAWvolution's Famous
>   Onion Bread (page 100)
> 1 cup chopped fresh basil
> 1 cup chopped fresh oregano
> 1 cup chopped portobello mushrooms, briefly marinated
>   in 1 or 2 tablespoons Nama Shoyu
> 1 cup chopped yellow onions
> 1 cup chopped red bell peppers
> 1 cup pitted and sliced Italian olives

Cut the collard green leaves into 4 squares with the same size as the bread.

Combine the Seed Cheese and Pizza Sauce in a small mixing bowl. Spread the mixture on the collard green squares, and place these on top of the Onion Bread squares. Sprinkle one fourth of the basil over each piece, covering it evenly. Repeat with the oregano, mushrooms, onions, bell peppers, and olives.

Shiitake Sandwich

Serves 1

A WHOLE MARINATED shiitake mushroom, crisp lettuce, onion, mustard, clover sprouts, and a thick slice of tomato served between two pieces of my Famous Onion Bread.

> 1 ½ teaspoons stone-ground mustard
>
> 2 to 3 lettuce leaves of your choice
>
> One 4 ¾-inch square piece of RAWvolution's Famous
>
>   Onion Bread (page 100), cut diagonally into 2 triangles
>
> 1 thin slice yellow onion
>
> 2 thick slices tomato
>
> 1 large shiitake mushroom, stem removed
>
> ¼ cup clover sprouts

Spread the mustard on the lettuce and place it on one triangle of the Onion Bread. Top with the onion, tomatoes, mushroom, sprouts, and the remaining Onion Bread triangle.

Falafel

Serves 3 to 4

SPROUTED AND DEHYDRATED chickpea croquettes seasoned with fresh herbs and Indian spices.

Scant ¾ cup sprouted chickpeas, ground
    in a food processor

¾ cup raw sunflower seeds, finely ground
    in a food processor

Scant ¾ cup raw almonds, finely ground
    in a food processor

¼ yellow onion, diced

¼ cup olive oil

2 tablespoons fresh lemon juice

⅓ cup Nama Shoyu

3 cloves garlic, peeled

2 tablespoons curry powder

In a mixing bowl, combine all of the ingredients and mix thoroughly. Using a 1½- to 2-ounce ice-cream scoop with a levered pinching handle, form the mixture into mounds on a dehydrator tray. Dehydrate at 100°F for approximately 32 hours.

SERVING SUGGESTION: Serve with Mango Chutney (page 116).

Falafel with Mango Chutney

Seed Cheese Wrap

Serves 2

1

SUNFLOWER SEED CHEESE, fresh cilantro and basil, clover sprouts, avocado, whole-leaf dulse, cherry tomatoes, scallions, and Italian olives in a collard green wrap.

½ cup Sunflower Seed Cheese (page 85)

2 medium collard green leaves

Handful of fresh basil

½ avocado, cut into cubes or slices

1 cup fresh cilantro leaves

2 cups clover sprouts

1 cup whole-leaf dulse

¾ cup chopped tomatoes

⅓ cup chopped scallions

¾ cup pitted and sliced Italian olives

Spread the seed cheese along the entire length of the collard greens. Top with layers of the basil, avocado, cilantro, clover sprouts, dulse, tomatoes, green onions, and olives.

Soft Taco with
Fresh Tomato Salsa

Serves 3 to 4

GROUND WALNUT MEAT seasoned with Mexican spices, encased in a collard green wrap and served with Fresh Tomato Salsa.

> 1 ½ cups raw walnuts, ground in a food processor
>
> 1 ½ teaspoons ground cumin
>
> ¾ teaspoon ground coriander
>
> 2 tablespoons Nama Shoyu
>
> 3 to 4 small or medium collard green leaves
>
> 1 cup shredded romaine lettuce
>
> 1 recipe Fresh Tomato Salsa (page 103)

In a small mixing bowl, combine the walnuts, cumin, and coriander, and mix well. Add the Nama Shoyu and mix well. Spread approximately ⅓ cup of the walnut mixture along the center stem of each collard green leaf, then add a layer of shredded lettuce. Top with approximately ⅓ cup of the salsa just before serving.

Spinach and Cheese Quiche

Serves 3

A FRESH SPINACH–AND–PINE NUT cheese filling served in a crust of my Famous Onion Bread.

FOR THE CRUST:

> 1 recipe RAWvolution's Famous Onion Bread (page 100),
>> mixed but not yet dehydrated

FOR THE FILLING:

> ¼ cup fresh lemon juice
>
> ¼ cup Nama Shoyu
>
> ¼ red bell pepper
>
> 2 cloves garlic, peeled
>
> 1 ½ cups raw pine nuts, macadamia nuts,
>> cashews, or a combination
>
> 2 cups chopped baby spinach
>
> ½ cup diced yellow onion

To make the crust, press the mixed batch of Onion Bread into 4-inch round crusts with a 1-inch high lip. Place on a Teflex-lined dehydrator tray and dehydrate at 100°F for 36 hours, removing the Teflex sheet after the first 24 hours.

IN A HIGH-SPEED BLENDER, combine all of the filling ingredients except the spinach and onion, and blend until smooth. Transfer to a small mixing bowl, add the spinach and onions, and mix well. Spoon the mixture into the crusts and serve.

Spinach and
Mushroom Quiche

Serves 3

A FRESH BABY SPINACH, portobello mushroom, and pine nut filling served in a crust of my Famous Onion Bread.

FOR THE CRUST:

> 1 recipe RAWvolution's Famous Onion Bread (page 100),
>   mixed but not yet dehydrated

FOR THE FILLING:

> ⅓ cup Nama Shoyu
>
> 2 cloves garlic, peeled
>
> 3 ½ cups portobello mushrooms
>
> 4 cups baby spinach
>
> ½ cup raw pine nuts

To make the crust, press the mixed batch of Onion Bread into 4-inch round crusts with a 1-inch high lip. Place on a Teflex-lined dehydrator tray and dehydrate at 100°F for 36 hours, removing the Teflex sheet after the first 24 hours.

In a food processor, combine all of the filling ingredients and blend thoroughly. Spoon the mixture into the crusts and serve.

Stir-Not-Fry

Serves 3 to 4

An AMAZING ARRAY of thinly sliced veggies in a sweet soy and ume vinegar marinade.

FOR THE SALAD:

½ cup shredded carrots

½ cup shredded zucchini

½ cup shredded daikon

1 head bok choy, stems chopped and leaves left whole

½ cup diced red bell peppers

½ cup shredded red cabbage

1 head broccoli, stems shredded, florets left whole

½ cup snow peas, cut in half crosswise

½ cup shredded parsnips

¼ cup scallions, cut diagonally

One 3-inch piece burdock root, cut into small discs (about ¼ cup)

¼ cup fresh parsley

1 tablespoon black or blonde raw sesame seeds

FOR THE DRESSING:

⅓ cup ume vinegar

⅓ cup Nama Shoyu

8 cloves garlic, peeled

One 1 ½-inch piece ginger, peeled

1 ¼ cups olive oil

In a mixing bowl, combine all of the salad ingredients and toss to mix thoroughly.

To make the dressing, in a high-speed blender, combine the vinegar, Nama Shoyu, garlic, and ginger. While the blender is running, pour in the olive oil in a slow, steady stream until the dressing has emulsified (you may not have used the full 1 ¼ cups). Pour over the salad, mix well, and serve.

Vegetable Lasagna

Serves 3 to 4

THINLY SLICED ZUCCHINI lasagna noodles topped with sun-dried tomato marinara, creamy Seed Cheese, fresh oregano, diced bell peppers, yellow onions, and marinated portobello mushrooms.

> ½ recipe Sunflower Seed Cheese (page 85)
> ½ recipe Marinara Sauce (page 73)
> 1 bunch fresh basil, stems removed and leaves chopped
> 1 bunch fresh oregano, stems removed and leaves chopped
> ⅓ cup diced yellow onions
> ½ cup diced red bell peppers
> ½ cup chopped portobello mushrooms, briefly marinated in
>   1 tablespoon Nama Shoyu
> 3 to 4 zucchini, sliced into long, flat pieces approximately ⅛ inch thick
>   on a mandoline slicer

In a medium mixing bowl, combine all of the ingredients except the zucchini and mix thoroughly.

Place 3 slices of zucchini side by side on a dehydrator tray, and cover evenly with some of the lasagna mixture. Top with another layer of zucchini and then another layer of lasagna mixture. Repeat until ingredients are gone. Serve as is or dehydrate at 100°F for 4 to 6 hours.

Veggie Cakes

Serves 3 to 4

TASTY, DEHYDRATED veggie-and-seed cakes with a mild flavor of the sea.

2 cups raw sunflower seeds, finely ground
   in a food processor
4 stalks celery, chopped
½ bunch scallions, chopped
1 ½ teaspoons dulse flakes
6 tablespoons fresh lemon juice
¼ cup olive oil
¼ cup Nama Shoyu
½ beet
1 to 2 cloves garlic, peeled

In a medium mixing bowl, combine the sunflower seeds, celery, green onions, and dulse flakes, and mix thoroughly.

In a high-speed blender, combine all of the remaining ingredients and blend until smooth.

Add the contents of the blender to the dry ingredients in the mixing bowl, and mix well with a spatula or wooden spoon. With your hands, form the mixture into round patties approximately ¾ inch thick and 2 ¾ inches in diameter. Place the patties on a dehydrator tray and dehydrate at 100°F for approximately 32 hours.

SERVING SUGGESTIONS: Serve with Creamy Dill Sauce (page 76) or Cocktail Sauce (page 70).

Nut Loaf

Serves 4

A HEARTY, textured, dehydrated nut-and-vegetable loaf.

1 ½ cups raw almonds, soaked for 3 to 4 hours, drained and dried

1 ½ cups raw walnuts, soaked for 3 to 4 hours, drained and dried

1 ½ cups raw sunflower seeds, soaked for 3 to 4 hours, drained and dried

2 ½ cups chopped portobello mushrooms, briefly marinated
   in 2 to 3 tablespoons Nama Shoyu

1 yellow onion, diced

3 cups chopped celery

½ bunch parsley, stems removed and leaves chopped

10 cloves garlic, minced

⅓ cup olive oil

2 tablespoons cumin seed

1 cup Nama Shoyu

½ bunch tarragon, stems removed and leaves chopped

½ teaspoon cayenne pepper

Using a Green Star juicer and the homogenizing attachment, homogenize the almonds, walnuts, and sunflower seeds. Transfer to a mixing bowl, add the remaining ingredients, and mix thoroughly, making sure to break apart any clumps.

Spread the mixture evenly on a dehydrator tray lined with Teflex sheet to a thickness of approximately 1 inch. Dehydrate at 100°F for 12 hours. Flip the tray over onto an empty tray, and gently peel the Teflex sheet off the nut loaf. Return to the dehydrator for another 20 hours.

VARIATION:

For nut loaf burger patties, form the mixture by hand into round patties approximately ½ inch thick and 2¾ inches in diameter. Dehydrate according to the directions above.

Tostada with Fresh Tomato Salsa

Serves 3

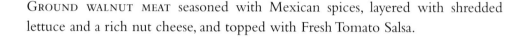

G<small>ROUND WALNUT MEAT</small> seasoned with Mexican spices, layered with shredded lettuce and a rich nut cheese, and topped with Fresh Tomato Salsa.

1 ½ cups raw walnuts, finely ground in a food processor

1 ½ teaspoons ground cumin

1 ½ teaspoons chili powder

¾ teaspoon ground coriander

2 tablespoons Nama Shoyu

1 cup shredded romaine lettuce

Three 4 ¾-inch square pieces RAWvolution's Famous
  Onion Bread (page 100)

1 recipe pierogi cheese filling (see page 119)

1 recipe Fresh Tomato Salsa (page 103)

In a small mixing bowl, combine the walnuts, cumin, chili powder, and coriander and mix well. Add the Nama Shoyu and mix well again.

Sprinkle about a third of the shredded lettuce on one piece of Onion Bread. Crumble about a third of the walnut mixture evenly over the lettuce, then top with about a third of the pierogi cheese. Repeat two more times with the remaining Onion Bread, walnut mixture, and pierogi cheese filling. Top each tostada with approximately ⅓ cup of salsa just before serving.

NINE

SUGAR ON
My Tongue

Desserts and Sweets

h, my favorite part of dinner—dessert! When I first moved to

California from Canada, raw chef Juliano, and I would split a raw apple pie

and eat it for breakfast. Life is sweet! I have always had a ravenous sweet

tooth, and I developed these recipes to help tame it. I always say, "Desserts

are easy—just make it sweet enough and everyone will love it!"

Nice Apple Tart

Serves 1 to 2

FRESH APPLES SLICES sweetened with raw agave nectar and whole raisins, spiced with ground cinnamon, and served in a sweet almond-meal crust.

FOR THE CRUST:

> 2 cups raw almonds, finely ground in a
>> food processor
>
> ⅓ cup agave nectar

FOR THE FILLING:

> 2 apples, cored
>
> 2 tablespoons agave nectar
>
> ½ teaspoon cinnamon, or ½ teaspoon apple pie spice
>
> 1 ½ teaspoons flax seed, ground in a food processor
>
> 1 ½ teaspoons fresh lemon juice
>
> ¼ cup raisins

To make the crust, in a mixing bowl, combine the ground almonds and agave nectar, and mix well. Press the mixture evenly into the bottom and sides of a 5-inch pie tin.

In a food processor, slice the apples with the slicing disc. Transfer to a mixing bowl, add the remaining ingredients, and mix well. Spoon the mixture into the pie crust and serve.

Almond Halvah

Makes about 20 balls

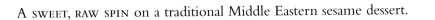

A SWEET, RAW SPIN on a traditional Middle Eastern sesame dessert.

> 1 cup raw tahini (half of a 16-ounce jar)
>
> ¾ cup agave nectar
>
> ¾ cup raw slivered almonds or whole almonds,
>   coarsely ground in a food processor
>
> ¾ cup raw almonds, finely ground in a food processor

In a mixing bowl, combine the tahini, agave nectar, and slivered or coarsely ground almonds and mix thoroughly.

Press the halvah into a glass baking dish. Coat with finely ground or slivered almonds. Cover and store in the freezer. Serve thoroughly chilled, right out of the freezer.

Coconut Fudge

Makes about 9 squares

A RICH CHUNK of walnut and coconut fudge sweetened with agave nectar.

3 cups raw walnuts
½ cup carob powder
2 cups shredded unsweetened coconut
⅝ cup agave nectar

Grind the walnuts in a food processor until they have a buttery consistency.

In a large mixing bowl, combine the carob powder and shredded coconut and mix well. Add the ground walnuts and the agave nectar and mix well.

Press the mixture into a glass baking dish, creating a flat, even layer approximately ¾ inch thick. Cut into squares and serve as is. Or cover and freeze until thoroughly chilled for a more solid consistency before cutting and serving.

Savoy Truffles

Makes about 20 truffles

RAW CAROB AND ALMOND TORTES sweetened with raw agave nectar and rolled in shredded coconut. In the RAWvolution kitchen, we call these Torte Balls. When my chef, Danny, began working for me he thought it was pronounced "tor-tay." It's pretty funny—so no one has corrected him yet.

2 cups raw almonds, finely ground
   in a food processor
½ cup carob powder
⅓ teaspoon sea salt (optional)

1 cup shredded unsweetened coconut
¾ cup agave nectar
2 tablespoons olive oil

In a mixing bowl, combine the almonds, carob powder, salt, and shredded coconut, and mix well. Add the agave nectar and olive oil and mix until a doughlike consistency is reached. Using your hands, roll the mixture into ping-pong-sized balls. Serve as is. Or cover and freeze before serving until thoroughly chilled for a more solid consistency.

Cinnamon Girls

Makes about 20 balls

SWEET, FRESHLY GROUND cinnamon-and-almond tortes with whole raisins, sweetened with raw agave nectar.

2 cups raw almonds, finely ground
   in a food processor

⅓ cup cinnamon

⅓ teaspoon sea salt (optional)

1 cup raisins

¾ cup agave nectar

2 tablespoons olive oil

In a medium mixing bowl, combine the almonds, cinnamon, salt, if using, and raisins, and stir until the dry ingredients are mixed well. Add the agave nectar and olive oil to the bowl, and mix until a doughlike consistency is reached. Using your hands, roll the mixture into ping-pong-sized balls. Serve as is, or cover and freeze before serving until thoroughly chilled for a more solid consistency.

Savoy Truffles (left) and Cinnamon Girls

Come Bite
the Apple Cookies

Makes about 20 cookies

RIPE RED APPLES, raisins, and ground cinnamon, sweetened with raw agave nectar and dehydrated into soft, homemade-style cookies.

> 2 pounds red apples, cored and peeled (5 to 6 apples, such as Fuji or Gala)
> 1 cup agave nectar
> 1 ¾ cups almonds, ground in a food processor
> 1 ¼ cups raisins
> ¼ cup cinnamon

In a food processor, slice half of the apples with the slicing disc. Transfer the sliced apples to a mixing bowl. Slice the remaining apples in the food processor with the shredding disc, then add the shredded apples to the sliced apples in the mixing bowl. Add the agave nectar, ground almonds, raisins, and cinnamon to the bowl, and mix well with a spatula.

With your hands, press the mixture into about 20 round, flat cookies approximately 3 inches thick, and lay them on dehydrator sheets. Dehydrate at 105°F for approximately 24 hours.

Coconut-Carob Haystacks

Makes about 16 haystacks

1

SHREDDED COCONUT, raw carob, and rich coconut butter sweetened with raw agave nectar and served in mini-haystacks.

½ cup carob powder

3 cups shredded unsweetened coconut

¾ cup coconut butter (sometimes called coconut oil)

½ cup agave nectar

In a medium mixing bowl, combine the carob powder and shredded coconut, and mix well. Add the coconut butter and agave nectar and mix well. Using an ice cream scoop, scoop into approximately 16 mounds. Freeze for at least 30 minutes before serving. The Haystacks can be stored in the freezer.

Sweet Virginia
Pecan Pie

Serves 1 to 2

A THICK RAISIN FILLING topped with whole raw pecans, served in a sweet almond meal crust.

FOR THE CRUST:

> 2 cups raw almonds, finely ground in a food processor
>
> ⅓ cup agave nectar

FOR THE FILLING:

> ⅓ cup coconut water
>
> ¼ cup pecans
>
> ½ cup raisins

To make the crust, in a mixing bowl, combine the ground almonds and agave nectar, and mix well. Press the crust mixture evenly into the bottom and sides of a 5-inch pie tin.

In a high-speed blender, combine all of the filling ingredients and blend until smooth. Spoon the mixture into the pie crust. Top with whole or chopped pecans and serve.

GARNISH:

¼ cup raw pecans, whole or chopped

Eat a Peach

Serves 1 to 2

FRESH SUMMER PEACH SLICES, sugared with raw agave nectar and served in a sweet almond-meal crust.

FOR THE CRUST:

2 cups raw almonds, finely ground in a food processor

⅓ cup agave nectar

FOR THE FILLING:

2 peaches, pitted

1 tablespoon agave nectar

To make the crust, in a mixing bowl, combine the ground almonds and agave nectar, and mix well. Press the mixture evenly into the bottom and up the sides of a 5-inch pie tin.

To ___ **filling,** in a food processor, slice the peaches using the slicing disc. Transfer ___ to a mixing bowl, and add the agave nectar. Mix well, then ___ the pie crust, and serve.

Persimmon Pie

Serves 1 to 2

A RICH Hachiya persimmon sauce served in a sweet almond-meal crust.

FOR THE CRUST:

    2 cups raw almonds, finely ground in a
        food processor
    ⅓ cup agave nectar

FOR THE FILLING:

    1 to 2 Hachiya persimmons

To make the crust, in a mixing bowl, combine the ground almonds and agave nectar, and mix well. Press the mixture evenly into the bottom and sides of a 5-inch pie tin.

To make the filling, in a high-speed blender, puree the persimmons. Pour into the pie crust and serve.

Pineapple Heart

Serves 1 to 2

BLENDED HAWAIIAN PINEAPPLE and fresh mango, topped with shredded coconut, and served in a sweet almond-meal crust.

FOR THE CRUST:

    2 cups raw almonds, finely ground in a
        food processor
    ⅓ cup agave nectar

FOR THE FILLING:

- ¾ cup mango cubes
- ¾ cup pineapple chunks
- ½ cup agave nectar
- 1 ½ cups raw macadamia or cashew nuts
- ¼ cup fresh lemon juice

To make the crust, in a mixing bowl, combine the ground almonds and agave nectar, and mix well. Press the mixture evenly into the bottom and sides of 5-inch pie tin.

In a high-speed blender, combine all of the filling ingredients and blend until smooth. Pour the mixture into the pie crust and serve.

GARNISH:

1 tablespoon shredded unsweetened coconut

Pineapple Heart

Spirulina Pie

Serves 1 to 2

THE HEALTHIEST—and greenest—pie ever to taste so good. Sometimes I make only the filling, freeze it, and eat it straight from the bowl.

FOR THE CRUST:

>   2 cups raw almonds, finely ground in a
>   food processor
>   ⅓ cup agave nectar

FOR THE FILLING:

>   ¾ cup Thai coconut water
>   ¼ cup raw cashews
>   ¼ cup coconut butter (sometimes called coconut oil)
>   ⅓ cup agave nectar
>   2 tablespoons spirulina
>   1 tablespoon carob powder

To make the crust, in a mixing bowl, combine the ground almonds and agave nectar, and mix well. Press the mixture evenly into the bottom and sides of a 5-inch pie tin.

In a high-speed blender, combine all of the filling ingredients and blend until smooth. Pour the mixture into the pie crust and freeze for approximately 1 hour before serving.

Strawberry Fields Forever

Serves 1 to 2

FRESH STRAWBERRIES SLICES, sugared with raw agave nectar and served in a sweet almond-meal crust.

FOR THE CRUST:

  2 cups raw almonds, finely ground in a
    food processor
  ⅓ cup agave nectar

FOR THE FILLING:

  1 ½ cups strawberries
  ¼ cup agave nectar

To make the crust, in a mixing bowl, combine the ground almonds and agave nectar, and mix well. Press the mixture evenly into the bottom and sides of a 5-inch pie tin.

To make the filling, in a food processor, slice the strawberries with the slicing disc. Transfer the sliced berries to a mixing bowl, add the agave nectar, and mix well. Spoon the mixture into the pie crust and serve.

TEN

SAMPLE Menus

Impress your family, friends, or lover by preparing a menu that is not only completely organic and raw, but that also perfectly fits the occasion. The dishes featured in this section were combined to both complement each other and create a complete and well-rounded meal. No matter what you're in the mood for, there will be something for you here!

●　　●　　●

AMERICAN

○ Thick 'N' Thin: Sprouted Lentil Chili (page 59)

○ Creamy Cabbage Coleslaw (page 88)

○ Sloppy Joe Sandwich (page 123)

○ Nice Apple Tart (page 161)

ASIAN

○ Siamese Dream Thai Curry Soup (page 56)

○ Thai Coleslaw (page 111)

○ Stir-Not-Fry (page 150)

○ Asian Vegetable Nori Rolls (page 129)

FRENCH

○ Glass Onion: French Onion Soup (page 41)

○ Organic Greens with Garlic Cream Dressing (page 70)

○ Spinach and Cheese Quiche (page 146)

○ Spinach and Mushroom Quiche (page 149)

HOLIDAY

ITALIAN

MEXICAN RAWVOLUTION

o Going to California Guacamole (page 95)

o Nopalito Cactus Salad (page 112)

o Soft Taco (page 145) or

  Tostada with Fresh Tomato Salsa (page 156)

MIDDLE EASTERN

o No-Bean Hummus (page 104)

o Mediterranean Tabouli (page 99)

o Cauliflower Couscous (page 83)

o Falafel (page 140)

o Mango Chutney (page 116)

o Almond Halvah (page 163)

PARTY HORS D'OEUVRES

o RAWvolution's Famous Onion Bread (page 100)

o Tapenade-Stuffed Shiitake Mushroom Caps (page 108)

o Cheese Pierogies (page 119)

ROMANTIC DINNER

o RAWvolution's Famous Onion Bread (page 100)

o Little Green Cream of Celery Soup (page 47)

o Maggie's Farm Marinated Greens (page 96)

o Zucchini Pasta Alfredo (page 130), Pasta Marinara

(page 132), or Pesto Pasta (page 133)

o Vegetable Lasagna (page 153)

o Spirulina Pie (page 179)

SEAFOOD

o Veggie Cakes (page 154)

o Cocktail Sauce (page 70)

o Octopus's Garden Seaweed Chowder (page 51)

o Organic Greens with Sweet Herb Oil Dressing made

with dill (page 75)

o Mock Tuna Salad

(page 126)

SUMMER BBQ/PICNIC

o Organic Greens with Creamy Ranch Dressing

  (page 67)

o Cucumber-Dill Salad (page 91)

o Summer Corn Salad (page 87)

o Egg-less Egg Salad (page 92)

o Big Matt with Cheese (page 125)

o Eat a Peach (page 175) or Strawberry Fields

  Forever (page 180)

ELEVEN

ON THE
Road Again

How to Eat Raw While Traveling

Since 1998, I have traveled extensively throughout the United States, Canada, and abroad, eating only raw foods. I've traveled by train, airplane, boat, and car on long road trips. I've been hostelling, camping, and in fine hotels. Finding good food while traveling can be a challenge. But the good news for you is that I've already done the research. Here's what you can do to make eating on the road easier.

HAVE ME MAKE IT!

Each week, my company RAWvolution creates boxes of prepared, organic raw foods. Each one includes two savory soups, four gourmet entrées, four side dishes, and two delicious desserts. You can bring the box with you on a flight, or have it shipped overnight to your destination anywhere in the continental United States. Pass on the airplane "food" and order The Box! To order, visit www.rawvolution. com. RAWvolution—We don't cook so you don't have to.

SHOP WHEN YOU ARRIVE!

Locate health food stores near where you will be staying before you leave on your trip. Bring this book with you. Prepare simple dishes in your hotel room or in your family or friends' kitchen. Share with them, and they may even clear a shelf for you in their refrigerator.

EAT OUT!

In Japanese or sushi restaurants, order a veggie hand roll without rice. Ask for lettuce, avocado, carrots, sprouts, cucumber, peppers, onions, or any other veggies you see on the menu. Some sushi restaurants also serve excellent cucumber or seaweed salads.

In Mexican restaurants, order a green salad, skip the dressing, and smother it in fresh salsa and guacamole.

Salads are great, and you can get one at even the most redneck steak house. Again, skip the dressing and croutons and ask for olive oil, half a lemon, and some freshly ground pepper. Iceberg lettuce never tasted so good!

Research raw food restaurants in the city or town where you will be traveling—they are sprouting up all over the country.

TAKE SOME TO GO!

Pack your bags with the following dehydrated recipes from this book. They won't spoil, and they will be satisfying additions to salads while you're away. Several desserts that travel well are also listed.

- Cheese Sticks (page 84)
- RAWvolution's Famous Onion Bread (page 100)
- Tapenade-Stuffed Shiitake Mushroom Caps (page 108)
- Falafel (page 140)
- Veggie Cakes (page 154)
- Nut Loaf (page 155)
- Almond Halvah (page 163)
- Coconut Fudge (page 164)
- Cinnamon Girls (page 166)
- Come Bite the Apple Cookies (page 169)
- Coconut-Carob Haystacks (page 170)
- Savoy Truffles (page 166)
- Berry and Nut Breakfast Bar (page 31)

GLOSSARY

Many of the following items can be found at your local health food store or online at www.rawfood.com.

Agave Nectar A very sweet syrup naturally extracted from the inner core of the blue agave (a cactus-like plant native to Mexico, best known for its use in making tequila). Agave nectar is absorbed slowly into the bloodstream, decreasing the highs and lows associated with sugar intake. It is unprocessed, and therefore provides vitamins and minerals not found in processed sweeteners.

Almond Butter A thick butter cold pressed from organic raw almonds.

Apple Cider Vinegar A vinegar made from aged apple cider. The vinegar is rich in enzymes and potassium and is said to improve digestion. Organic, raw, unpasteurized, and unfiltered is best. Available at heath food stores.

Apple Pie Spice A spice blend usually containing cinnamon, nutmeg, allspice, and/or cardamom.

Basil An aromatic herb native to India and associated with Italian, Indian, and Asian cuisines. Varieties include Italian, opal (or purple), lemon, and Thai.

Bok Choy An East Asian leafy vegetable related to the Western cabbage, with smooth, dark-green leaf blades forming a cluster reminiscent of celery.

Cacao Butter The pure, cold-pressed oil of the cacao (chocolate) bean. White chocolate is made of cacao butter.

Cacao Nibs The peeled and broken seeds (or beans) of the cacao fruit. All chocolate is made from the cacao bean. The beans were so revered by the Mayans and

Aztecs that they used them as money! Cacao is remarkably rich in magnesium and seems to diminish the appetite, probably due to its monoamine oxidase enzyme inhibitors (MAO inhibitors).

Cacao Powder A real raw chocolate powder made from the cacao bean.

Carob Powder A coarse powder derived from carob, a brown, pod-shaped fruit native to Mediterranean countries. Carob powder is used as a chocolate substitute and contains no caffeine.

Cashews The fruit of an evergreen tree native to the Amazon region. The cashew is a relative of both the mango and the pistachio. Cashews are often erroneously considered poisonous unless roasted. Raw cashews are rich in magnesium, phosphorus, and potassium.

Cayenne A very spicy seasoning made from dried cayenne peppers.

Chard A leafy green vegetable with large, broad leaves that are slightly salty. They are rich in chlorophyll as well as calcium, iron, potassium, and sulfur.

Chili Powder A spice blend usually containing paprika, cayenne, cumin, garlic, and oregano.

Chives An herb and a member of the onion family. This plant with thin, tubular leaves is native to Asia. The leaves have a flavor reminiscent of onion, and they are often confused with scallions.

Cilantro Known also as "coriander" or "Chinese parsley," this aromatic herb is most associated with Mexican and Asian cuisine.

Cinnamon Once more valuable than gold, cinnamon is a powder, ground from the inner bark of a tree in the laurel family. It has a warm, sweet flavor and is used in both savory and sweet dishes.

Clover Sprouts The immature plant of the clover seed (a legume). Sprouts are truly a living food. Even after you have harvested them, they will continue to grow slowly, and their vitamin content will actually increase. Sprouts are the most enzyme-rich food that exists.

Coconut Butter The oil pressed from the flesh of coconuts. Sometimes called "coconut oil," coconut butter contains up to 50 percent medium-chain saturated fatty acids, which have powerful antibacterial, antimicrobial, and anti-fungal properties. Coconut butter has cholesterol-lowering properties, is an instant energy source, contains no cholesterol or trans-fatty acids, and is not hydrogenated.

Collard Greens This leafy green vegetable is a mineral-rich member of the cabbage family. It has large, flat leaves, which are perfect for using in place of tortillas for wraps.

Coriander A spice ground from the seeds of the cilantro plant, used primarily in Indian and Mexican cuisine.

Cumin A seed used whole or ground to produce a powdered spice that appears primarily in Indian and Mexican cuisine.

Curry Powder A spice blend usually containing turmeric, cumin, coriander, cayenne, and cardamom. It is used primarily in Indian cuisine.

Daikon Radish From the Japanese words *dai* ("large") and *kon* ("root"), this large, white root vegetable has a juicy, crunchy texture and pungent taste.

Dill This aromatic herb is a member of the parsley family, and is popular in Asian and Persian cuisine.

Dulse (Whole-Leaf) Reddish-purple seaweed with flat, fan-shaped fronds that grows from the temperate to frigid zones of the Atlantic and Pacific Oceans. This alkaline vegetable is an excellent source of iron, potassium, iodine, and manganese. This seaweed is soft and dry and keeps for many months.

Dulse Flakes or Granules A coarsely ground powder made from dried, whole-leaf dulse.

Flax Seeds Tiny brown or yellow seeds rich in essential fatty acids, calcium, iron, magnesium, potassium, and vitamin E. Available at health food stores.

Food Dehydrator A low-temperature "oven" used to gently dry fruit or prepared raw dishes, creating drier, heartier textures while maintaining nutritional integrity. Excalibur is the brand I recommend.

Food Processor An appliance that makes quick work of chopping and shredding vegetables and grinding nuts and seeds.

Garam Masala From the Indian words *garam* ("warm") and *masala* ("mix"), this spice mix, which has dozens of variations, is used widely in Indian food.

Garlic Press A hand-held device used to crush cloves of peeled garlic.

Ginger This aromatic rhizome has a pungent flavor and is used mainly in Asian and Indian cuisine.

Goji Berries The Goji berry is a deep-red fruit that is picked and then dried before consumption. A dried Goji berry is a little smaller than a raisin, and is perhaps the most nutritionally rich fruit on the planet. Goji berries contain eighteen kinds of amino acids, including all eight essential amino acids, and up to twenty-one trace minerals. They are the richest source of carotenoids, including beta-carotene, of all the known plants on earth! Gojis contain 500 times more vitamin C by weight than oranges, and they also contain vitamins B_1, B_2, B_6, and vitamin E. Goji berries are regarded in Eastern medicine as a longevity food of the highest order.

Greek Olives These sun-cured olives are packed in cold-pressed extra virgin olive oil and sea salt. They are raw and unsprayed.

Green Powders Green powders are a raw food multivitamin to be taken on a daily basis especially during periods of cleansing or fasting. The best varieties contain a combination of raw, organic, and wild-crafted greens and cereal grasses, algae, aquatic vegetables, digestive enzymes, and probiotics (designed to implant good bacteria in the intestines). Nature's First Food, Pure Synergy, Dr. Greens, and Catie's are some of the very best.

Hachiya Persimmon A sweet, orange-skinned fruit with a jamlike flesh. It's ready to be eaten once it has become extremely soft.

Hemp Protein Powder Made from raw organic hemp seeds, hemp protein is a balanced, whole protein, rich in essential fatty acids, amino acids, vitamins, minerals, and antioxidants. Unlike other protein powders, it naturally contains the perfect balance of omega-3 and omega-6 fatty acids, and boasts twenty-two grams of protein per serving! Ideal for vegan athletes and growing vegan kids!

Hemp Seeds Hemp seeds (or hemp nuts) look like sesame seeds and have a nutty flavor. Hemp seeds contain 33 percent pure digestible protein and are rich in iron and vitamin E as well as omega-3 and omega-6 essential fatty acids.

High-Speed Blender Any commercial-style blender with a 2 horsepower (or larger) motor. Vita-Mix is the brand that I recommend.

Horseradish Root A spicy root from the mustard family.

Italian Olives These pitted olives are packed in pure water with a dash of fresh garlic, a dash of fresh oregano, one ripe cayenne pepper, and a dash of Celtic sea salt. They are raw and unsprayed.

Jicama (He-ka-ma) A tuberous root vegetable used extensively in Mexico. Its crunchy white flesh is less starchy than a potato, has a mildly sweet flavor, and is very juicy.

Juice Extractor A machine that separates the juice from the fiber of vegetables and fruits. The Green Star is the one that I recommend, as it is very efficient in extracting the maximum amount of juice without exposing it to any heat.

Kale This leafy green vegetable is a mineral-rich member of the cabbage family.

Lucuma Powder Made from a maple-flavored fruit that has long been a culinary favorite in Peru, where lucuma-flavored ice cream is more popular than chocolate! Lucuma is a great source of beta-carotene, niacin, and iron.

Maca Root Powder Maca's history as a powerful strength and stamina enhancer and libido/fertility herb stretches back well over 500 years. Maca is a powerful adaptogen, which means it has the ability to balance and stabilize the body's systems. It can raise low blood pressure as well as lower high blood pressure. It is also high in iron and iodine.

Mandoline Slicer Allows you to cut and slice safely and quickly with a controlled back-and-forth motion over a V-shaped stainless steel blade. Slices fruits and vegetables to your desired thickness.

Mesquite Powder A traditional Native American food produced by gathering ripened seedpods from the mesquite tree and grinding them into a fine powder. Used as a staple food for centuries by desert dwellers, this high-protein meal is also high in calcium, magnesium, potassium, iron and zinc, and is rich in the amino acid lysine. It has a sweet, rich, molasseslike flavor with a hint of caramel.

Mint An aromatic herb most associated with Asian, Indian, and Persian cuisine.

Mustard Greens This leafy green vegetable is a mineral-rich member of the cabbage family and is also rich in natural sulphur.

Nama Shoyu Known as "the champagne of soy sauces," this organic, unpasteurized Japanese soy sauce is aged in wooden kegs.

Nopalitos One of two foods derived from the prickly pear cactus (the other is the prickly pear, or cactus fruit). *Nopal* means "cactus" in Spanish. The term *Nopalitos* refers to the pads once they have been cut up and prepared for eating.

Nori Square sheets of dried seaweed typically used for making sushi. The black sheets are raw, and the green are toasted.

Nut-Milk Bag A fine-mesh bag, usually with a drawstring. Used for straining juices and nut milks.

Nutmeg A spice powder ground from the seed of the nutmeg tree.

Olive Oil The "juice" of the olive fruit. This rich oil is best when it is organic and stone-pressed, which is superior to cold-pressed oil. The latter is often extracted at a heat of up to 240°F.

Oregano A member of the mint family, this aromatic herb is used extensively in Italian and Mexican cuisine.

Parsley Often looked upon as a mere garnish, this aromatic herb is popular in Persian and Italian cuisine. Varieties include Italian (flat-leaf) and curly parsley.

Pastry Bag Used to pipe semisolid foods by pressing them through a narrow opening at one end, especially for cake decoration. The bag is filled through the wider opening at the opposite end, rolled or twisted closed, and then squeezed to release its contents in a controlled manner.

Pure Water Any filtered, distilled, reverse osmosis, or artesian spring water.

Rosemary A member of the mint family. The leaves of this shrub are commonly used in Italian cuisine, including bread.

Sage An aromatic herb with strongly flavored leaves.

Sea Salt Harvested by hand using the 2,000-year-old tradition of salt farming. There is no comparison, in taste or in health effects, between the hand-harvested, mineral-rich sea salts and the modern, iodized salt that is treated with chemicals to allow it to flow freely and maintain a stark white color. Sea salt is dried by the sun and the wind, but retains the ocean's moisture, which helps to lock in many vital trace elements.

Shredded Coconut A product of the mature coconut. Sweet in flavor and rich in healthy oils that are antibacterial, antifungal, and antimicrobial.

Spatula A tool with a soft rubber edge that helps you to efficiently empty a blender or bowl. Not the metal kind you flip burgers with.

Spirooli Slicer A three-in-one turning slicer with stainless steel blade inserts that slices, shreds, and chips raw vegetables.

Spirulina A fine powder dried from blue-green algae offering an amazing array of vitamins, minerals, and phytonutrients, this micro-algae is 60 percent all-vegetable protein, rich in beta-carotene, iron, vitamin B_{12}, and rare essential fatty acids.

Sprouted Chickpeas Chickpeas, also known as "garbanzo beans," that have been soaked in water, drained, and left to germinate, thus rendering them edible without cooking. Available (both dry and sprouted) in health food stores.

Sprouted Lentils (Red or Green) Lentils are legumes that are often cooked before they are eaten. They can also be purchased sprouted which makes them edible without being cooked. Sprouting lentils involves soaking them for several hours in water, draining them and then allowing them to germinate or sprout.

Stone-Ground Mustard A natural type of prepared mustard made with mustard seeds, apple cider vinegar, and sea salt. Available in health food stores.

Sun-Dried Tomatoes Sliced tomatoes that are dried naturally in the sun. Sun-dried tomatoes can be purchased in health food stores and farmers markets. Or you can dry your own on a sunny day or, alternatively, in a food dehydrator.

Sunflower Sprouts The immature plant of the sunflower seed. Sprouts are truly a living food. Even after you have harvested them, they will continue to grow slowly, and their vitamin content will actually increase. Sprouts are the most enzyme-rich food that exists.

Tahini A smooth, thick butter made from hulled sesame seeds. Tahini is popular in Middle Eastern cuisine and is rich in both calcium and protein.

Tarragon An aromatic herb with a flavor mildly reminiscent of anise.

Teflex Sheet Solid, nonstick, reusable sheets made from Teflon to be used when drying wet items in an Excalibur food dehydrator.

Thai Coconut Water The water found within the young Thai coconut. Thai coconut water is one of the highest sources of electrolytes and has the same electrolytic balance as our blood. It also contains potassium, sodium, calcium, phosphorous, iron, copper, and sulphur.

Thyme An aromatic herb. Varieties include English, French, lemon, and lime.

Turmeric A spice ground from a dried root in the ginger family. It is a significant ingredient in most curry powders.

Ume Vinegar A treasured by-product from the traditional process of pickling umeboshi plums with sea salt and shiso leaves. This vinegar is ruby-red, tangy, and quite salty in taste.

Vanilla Bean The hand-cultivated fruit pod of the vanilla orchid (the only fruiting orchid). Vanilla flavor in its most natural and delectable form.

Wakame A tasty sun-dried seaweed that expands significantly when soaked in water.

ACKNOWLEDGMENTS

My most heartfelt thanks to the following people and organizations for their help on this book:

Janabai; George, Rose, Crystal, Jonny, Ruth and Donna Amsden; Eric Brent; Jenny Brown; Piter Caizer; Rich Cashman; Ryan Couture; Carla Cummings; Kerrie Cushing; Michael Davis; Dr. Richard DeAndrea; Nicole Dionne; Bill, Sahaja, Liam, and Aiden Douglass; Dwight Durham; Andrea Gomez; Anneliese Gomez de Costello; Bobbi Goodman; Jason Hiller; Heath House; Declan Joyce; Juliano; Don Kidson; Whitney Landau; Karl Lindstrom; Alison Lohman; Elaina Love; Craig and Sean MacFayden; Liesl Maggiore; Isa Metcalf; Vernon and Linda Myers; Sergio Nicolas; Maureen O'Neal; Nick Owens; Cathy and Dave Phillion; Judith Regan; Maureen Regan; Melissa Remark; Danny Snodgrass; Sean Snodgrass; Alison Stoltzfus; Joshua Townsend-Zellner; Star Townsend-Zellner-Lindstrom; Joe and Geraldine Trahan; Len Weschler; Steve and Mookie White; David Wolfe; and Dr. John Wood.

California Organic Fruits, Coleman Family Farm, Maggie's Farm, Munak Ranch, Rain Farms, Laura Ramirez, Rivas Farms, Sycamore Hills Farm, Tutti Frutti Farms, Weiser Farms, and David West.

Crate & Barrel and Sur La Table.

INDEX

207